"The Legal Method" To Clearing Your Own Credit

Secrets the credit bureaus don't want you to know

Learn the laws that are in your favor

See (POSITIVE?) results within 45 days

You can do this

Seek and you will find.
knock and the door will be open.
Matthew 7: 7

Sherri Vanderpool

"The Legal Method" To Clearing Your Own Credit

By Sherri Vanderpool

Copyright © 2010

Registered with the Library of Congress

Printed in the United States of America

Vanderpool, Sherri

> *"The Legal Method" To Clearing Your Own Credit* / by Sherri Vanderpool
> ISBN: 978-0-615-34935-0

All rights reserved. Except for use in a review, no portion of this book may be reproduced in any form without the express written permission of the author.

The author assumes no responsibility for the use or misuse of information contained in this book.

Warning

This book contains certain confidential information that could easily be subject to abuse or misuse. The guidelines used in the forms are according to the Federal Trade Commission and Fair Debt Collection Practices Act.

This is not a law book but rather a means to use the laws that are available to the public for the repairing and correcting of one's own credit.

The author is not rendering any legal service or advice.

The services of a professional are recommended if legal advice or assistance is needed. The author is not responsible for personal loss or liabilities caused by the use or misuse of any information presented herein.

To my wonderful friend and Editor Ginger Tafoya, thank you so much for all your wonderful help in putting this book together, I could not have done this without you. I look forward to working with you on future projects.

To my three lovely daughters Amber, Erin, and Stephanie you have always been an inspiration in my life. Without your love and support this book would not have been possible.

TABLE OF CONTENTS

Table of Contents 5
Introduction 7
Chapter 1: Credit and You the Consumer 9
How Inquiries Work 11
How to Maintain Good Credit 12
How To Make Changes And Corrections To Your Credit Report 18
Obtaining a Free Copy of Your Credit Reports 19
Chapter 2: Bankruptcy 21
Form Letters to use after filing Bankruptcy 25
Bankruptcy 25
Cease and Desist 26
Chapter 3: Collections 31
Collection Accounts Listed with a Collection Agency 31
The Seven-year Rule 33
What is a Collection Agency 37
What is Sale of Debt 38
The Fair Debt Collection Practices Act 38
Example of Letters for Your Use 42
In The Senate Of The United States 45
Privacy 46
In Conclusion 47
Cease and Desist 50
Debt Validation Verification 52
Debt Validation And Verification 54
Chapter 4: Statute of Limitations 61
Contracts 62
The "Statute of Limitations" is Vital in the World of Credit 63
Keeping Good Records to Prove Your Statute of Limitations 64
Your Goal is to Stop Duplicate Reporting 65
Statute of Limitations in Your State 66
Statute of Limitations Chart by State 67
Chapter 5: Asking for Forgiveness or Verification from your Creditors 71
How to Ask Forgiveness or Verification for an Account 71
Enhancing Your Credit Score 73
Forgiveness of Debt Document 73
Forgiveness of Late Payment on an Open Account Document 73
Forgiveness of a Late Payment on a Paid Off Account Document 74
Verification of a Debt 74
F.O.L, also known as: Forgiveness of Late payment. 76

Forgiveness of Late 76
Student Loans 81
The Student Loan Hook 81
The Truth.. 82
Canceling a Student Loan 82
Getting Out of Default 83
Steps to Rectify a Default 84
A Deferment 85
A Forbearance 85
Why and How to Correct Student Loan Issues on Your Credit File 85
F.O.L Student Loans. 88
Chapter 7: Breaking a Lease Auto, Home or Apartment 89
Break a Lease? Impossible, You Say... 89
Car Lease.. 90
Home or Apartment Lease 91
Chapter 8: The IRS 97
The Internal Revenue Service 97
There is Hope 97
It Never Hurts to Try... 99
Chapter 9: Disputes with Credit Bureaus 101
Updating vs. Disputing Credit Bureaus Overview 102
How to Dispute Accounts with each Credit Bureau......................... 103
Experian Dispute Letter 108
Collection Agency Accounts... 110
Debt Validation and Verification Letter #1 112
Debt Validation Verification Letter #2 114
Other Negative Accounts on Your Credit Report 116
What to do When Your Credit Reports Come Back from the Credit Bureaus .122
How to get More Accounts Deleted the Second Time Around 125
Request to Seal Records 130
Cease and Desist 143
Once a Credit Report Comes Back Reflecting that all Accounts have been Verified .146
Chapter 10: Inquiry Removal 153
Experian Report 155
Transunion Report... 157
Equifax Report 159
Forms 163

Introduction

It's a well know fact that many employers conduct credit checks on prospective job applicants prior to hiring. Some employers also perform random credit checks on employees to determine those who are worthy of keeping their current position.

The point is that we must consciously admit that credit significantly affects us all. Therefore, we must treat credit with respect if we want to maintain or improve our standard of living. If we want to be able to take advantage of life's opportunities, credit is a general necessity.

As we consider credit and how it affects us and our everyday lives, we can see that we are living in credit-driven society.

We all fit into one of two categories of Americans:

Category 1: People with **GOOD** credit

Category 2: People with **NO** credit or, worse, with **BAD** credit

At some point in our lives, most of us have had bad experiences concerning our creditworthiness. According to a recent national survey, about 70 percent of American adults have some type of derogatory information on their credit reports. These derogatory items have not necessarily been caused by direct, negligent action on the part of the individual. Some items occurred because of job layoffs, medical emergencies and unfortunate economic difficulties such as the recession of 2007-2009. During such times, having good credit might prove to be a lifesaver; on the other hand, large credit payments may further stretch already tight finances.

Regardless of circumstances, we remain responsible for our own creditworthiness. It will be affected by how we handle our credit in response to the situations confronting us.

Credit is important to livelihood and quality of life: In the short, tight spots of life, it may very well mean continued survival.

We can reap the benefits of credit in this society only when we take it upon ourselves to create good credit in our name.

CHAPTER 1

Credit and You the Consumer

*M*any consumers today are being taken advantage of because they lack credit knowledge. This book will inform you of your rights and how the law will protect you in regaining your credit once again.

People today are highly in debt with mortgages, autos, loans and credit cards. Disaster strikes when the unforeseen happens with a general layoff due to a company downsizing or a person is dismissed from his/her company.

So what are people to do with the monthly bills that they has have always paid on time now that the family income has dropped to below half—unemployment does not sufficiently compensate the lost income.

With a lower income causing enough stress, now you have the creditors to contend with. They are demanding the payment still be paid and on time. You explain your situation, and they won't budge. They want their money. In some cases, creditors will work with you for a couple months, giving you the option of making interest-only payments. This will help to keep your account from being reported to the credit bureaus. *However*, the interest-only payments will now be added on to the end of your contract, which will add a few months to the length you were originally supposed to pay.

A Double Whammy

Some creditors who have opted not to work with you begin sending your accounts to collectors. They also will report to the credit bureaus, causing your credit to be damaged.

The same account can then be reported again by a collection agency that either bought the account or was given the account from the original creditor, who did not want to be bothered with trying to collect this debt. They instead choose to write it off as a loss.

Your Rights

Information for this book was obtained with the help and guidance of the following:

- *Consumer Affairs*
- *Better Business Bureau*
- *Federal Trade Commission*
- *Fair Debt Collections Act*

You as a consumer will be amazed at what rights you have. Of course, no credit bureau wants you to know because it makes money on your financial problems.

All three credit bureaus receive money each time a creditor wants information about your credit file. They must pay the credit bureaus for the report.

How Inquiries Work

Each time a credit report is pulled up by a potential creditor, it will place a damaging mark against your FICA score— causing an inquiry to be revealed. If your credit is good and an account is opened, then your report will reflect open and it will raise your FICA score.

Let's say you want to purchase a new vehicle. You look at autos until you find one that you decide you want to pay for over the next 60 months—or even longer with the price of vehicles in today's market.

1. The salesman and you go into his office where he has you fill out a credit application.
2. You sign your name at the bottom, giving them permission to run a credit report, notice I said, "a" credit report. Back in the old days "a" meant one.
3. This dealership wants you to drive away in a new vehicle so it can make its quota and money for the day.
4. So by signing your name and not stating to the salesman that you only want your credit report run once, they proceed to send your application to many different financial institutions. This will cause each bank to run a credit report on you.

5. If the application is sent to 10 banks, your credit report will show inquiries 10 different times.

This does not look good, as it will reflect being turned down nine times. This will damage your FICA score.

Inquiries will remain on your credit report for a length of two years. Each time a creditor runs a report on you, an inquiry is placed on your report.

How to Maintain Good Credit

- Never apply for more credit than you need, i.e. House, auto and maybe one credit card to use in an emergency.

- Do not become an impulse buyer. Leave the credit cards at home in a safe place. Wait at least 24-hours before deciding to use the credit card for the purchase. Chances are, after this time, you will decide you either did not really need the item or it is just something you cannot live without.

> **TIP:** Instead of paying interest, you could use this extra money to put away for retirement years by using a good investment, such as an IRA retirement account or government bonds for your children's college education as these bonds do mature.

- Use the credit card only if you have the means to pay it off in full when your statement comes in. You do not want to waste your hard-earned money paying 18 – 24 percent interest just because you want to purchase these items now. *Be patient.*

- Put yourself on a budget, keep simple records and stick to it!

EXAMPLE:

			CALENDAR			
Monday	Tuesday	Wednesday	Thursday	Friday	Saturday	Sunday
1 Rent $500	2	3	4	5	6 Savings $25	7
8	9	10 Truck Pmt $790	11	12 Electric $125	13 Savings $25	14
15 Auto Ins $300	16	17	18	19	20 Savings $25	21
22	23 Cable TV $40	24	25	26	27 Savings $25	28

Purchase a calendar at any stationary store, preferably one that looks like a notebook, so you can put it in a specific drawer with your bills. You will be in total control of your budget with everything organized together and not wondering where you put your bills.

Your budgetary calendar is based on weekly paychecks every Friday. Depending on your paydays, first pay yourself, usually 15 percent of your take-home pay. You deserve it, so put in your saving account.

Can I Afford to be on a Budget?

You're most likely thinking, I can't afford it. Trust me, you will be surprised at how you can afford it.

Each month, mark your calendar when your bills arrive in the mail *NOT* when they are due. This way you will know around how much will be due for that particular week.

1. On your payday, you will be prepared to write out your checks for the bills you know will be arriving.
2. Pay them the day they arrive.
3. Keep plenty of stamps handy so actually mailing them will not be a problem.
4. If you work a few hours overtime, you now know exactly where that money will go on whatever you want.

This will be the best way to build your credit. You will not be tempted to overspend as you will be excited about the freedom from stress you are now living.

There are many books you can pick-up at the public library or book store to help with a budget.

What a Budget Can Do for You

Once you understand the importance of how to maintain good credit, for instance, you will be able to:

- Purchase a home with great interest and possibly 100% financing.

- Buy a car with 0-5% interest and sometimes with no down payment.
- Better rate with insurance as most insurance companies require a credit report.
- And most of all, have peace of mind.

It's All about Baby Steps with Want and Need

People do not necessarily enjoy being in debt. Yet many people have continually made impulse purchases, meaning they want it now and do not want to start a savings for this item. What they're not realizing is, they might not really want and need this item after all, or they have found something they needed to spend their money instead. Of course, a large purchase such as a house or vehicle might be a good idea to purchase on credit.

NOTE: Be smart and have only one credit card for an emergency, remembering to pay this credit card off in full before you're charged interest. Never use this card if you don't have the means to pay it off after each month.

With the following steps, you will be able to "see light at the end of the tunnel."

Gather together all your current bills, collection notices and past due bills. List each debt, balance due and balance past due.

FOR EXAMPLE:

BILL	CURRENT	PAST DUE
Electric	$146	
Ford Motor	$725	
Cell Phone		$250
Cable TV		$225
Auto Insurance	$355	
Visa credit card		$285
Mortgage (or rent)		$2,058

Great! See this task was not difficult. What was hard was seeing it on paper. If you are like most people, your heart was racing and you were uncomfortable writing down the past due accounts.

Notice the bills that are in the Current column and the bills in the Past Due column.

1. Decide if each item is a want or a need—meaning do you have it for need or pleasure

2. If the item is a need, figure out a way to keep it, but cut down on it. i.e. If it is the electric bill, there are ways to cut this down.

    a. Turn off all unused light. We know that children love to enter a room, turn on the lights and then leave without turning off the light.

    b. Purchase low energy light bulbs. Each bulb can save you up to $40 per year.

3. Next is the "cell phone," which is behind in payment by $250.

    a. Is this cell phone a need or want?

    b. You can purchase a cell phone and add minutes as you need them, such as a pre-paid cell phone.

    c. You can cut down on your minute usage. Sometimes let the callers go to voice mail. This gives you the opportunity to call from a landline, eliminating the usage of cell phone minutes.

4. The next bill in the past due category is a visa credit card bill.

    a. Try calling this credit card company to see if it is possible to reduce the interest on the card as this will lower your payments.

    b. Ask if they will reduce your payments temporarily for you to get caught up.

    c. Whatever creative way you can think of will be much to your advantage.

5. Your rent

    a. Go to your landlord ask if you can work out a way to keep living where you are, and make payments on your back rent while you keep the rent current from now on. You never know if you don't ask.

6. Your mortgage

    a. Call your mortgage company see if they have a program to help you get your mortgage caught up. The mortgage industry has many programs to help home owners keep there house.

The following are government facilities to offer help in time of need.

Freddie Mac: **Washington, DC**
Government & Industry Relations
401 9th Street, NW
Suite 600 South
Washington, DC 20004
www.freddiemac.com
202.434.8600
Fannie Mae: 800.7Fannie (732-6643)
9 a.m. – 5 p.m. Eastern Standard Time
www.fanniemae.com

How To Make Changes And Corrections To Your Credit Report

Most Americans believe the credit bureaus are 100 percent accurate. Wrong!

Credit bureaus report for tens of millions of people every year. And, yes, they make mistakes as human error does occur. In some instances, another person, with a similar name to yours, can end up on your file along with his/her social security number. This is why an account that you do not recognize will be on your file. It means the files have merged. Don't panic, this can be taken care of as long as you know what is on your credit file—which most people are not even aware of.

You can receive a free copy of your credit report once a year whether you have been denied credit or not. If you have already received your free copy for the physical year, you are entitled to a free report if you have been turned down for credit within the past 60 days.

OBTAINING A FREE COPY OF YOUR CREDIT REPORTS

If a bank has denied you a loan, it will send you a denial letter. Once you receive this, all you need to do is call or write to each credit bureau, notifying them that you have been denied credit. This will entitle you to a free updated credit report.

Trans Union, Equifax and Experian will send you a free copy of your credit report. It will list all inquiries with names, addresses and phone numbers that you will need to complete this task.

Experian	**Trans Union**	**Equifax**
P.O. Box 2002	P.O. Box 1000	P.O. Box 740241
Allen, TX 75013	Chester, PA 19022	Atlanta, GA 30374
888.397.3742	800.888.4213	800.685.1111

When contacting them, for your convenience, a form letter is in the back of this book.

Or if you would like to view and print your reports immediately, the credit bureaus have a central source at **www.annualcreditreport.com** or you can call their toll free number at: 877.322.8228

CHAPTER 2

Bankruptcy

This chapter is for anyone who has *already filed* a bankruptcy.

Before sending out any documents to any of the three major credit bureaus, get a current copy of your credit reports to see exactly what is on each one. After reviewing them, make a dispute with each credit bureau once your bankruptcy has been dismissed.

When you dispute each credit bureau, you will want to address each account that is listed in your bankruptcy.

This will ensure they are being correctly placed on your report. Make sure all accounts that have been filed in bankruptcy are actually being reported correctly, because these accounts will be hurting your credit score if they are still reporting negatively on your reports. This means that they are still being reported as any of the following:

- Charge off
- Placed in collections
- Repossession
- Foreclosure
- Transferred to another lender

Once you have disputed the items, the credit bureau will mail you an updated report within 30-45 days.

When you receive this, notice these accounts that you disputed will be reflecting the update now as:

- Account in Bankruptcy Chapter 7 or whatever chapter has been filed on your account.

You will see each account listed from each of your prior creditors who you have disputed. They will now be listing the accounts in bankruptcy as this is what your goal was to do.

If these accounts are still not reflecting in the bankruptcy, it would be a good idea then to mail a copy of the bankruptcy papers to each individual credit bureau with a list of each account that was entered into the bankruptcy, because the credit bureaus will need this proof to correctly update your credit file.

Remember: *Do not* send the credit bureaus your bankruptcy papers first. Your goal is to get as many accounts put in bankruptcy from the bureaus as you can without them receiving this paperwork.

It is only in your best interest if it is done this way first, as you will see later in this chapter the reasons why.

If your accounts have already been placed in bankruptcy, then you are one step ahead of correcting your own credit.

Important Note:

After your accounts have been listed in the bankruptcy for 24 months, it has been understood that some people have tried to dispute these same accounts again. Only this time, instead of disputing them as "in bankruptcy" like the first time, they thought to dispute them as "not mine," because these accounts are no longer yours as they have been a dead account for 24 months after the bankruptcy was filed.

Remember, you didn't send them your bankruptcy papers first; therefore, they have no copy of any bankruptcy to refer to. This is why you didn't want to send your bankruptcy papers first.

It is fine if you sent the bankruptcy papers after your first dispute.

During this process, the goal will be to get these accounts completely deleted, as it really should not be listed on your credit report because you have already given the account to the bankruptcy court.

The creditors have already dismissed and written off the accounts that were listed during this process and agreed that you no longer owed on these debts because they no longer are your responsibility. These accounts, as others believe, should not be on your report, but are listed in the "Public Records" section of the report as bankruptcy filed.

Then all other accounts that will be listed will only be your new current accounts, which are now giving you a positive credit rating.

Can you imagine having your credit report reflect only a "bankruptcy" listed in the public records section, and then, only good accounts listed in your current report? Wow, you will have an awesome credit score with the way your report is now being viewed.

Isn't this your No. #1 goal, with working to clear up your credit? As most people believe, you can do this with all three credit bureaus until you get the results you are working so hard to achieve.

Form Letters to Use After Filing Bankruptcy

Use this document after you have filed a bankruptcy. Send a copy to each creditor who is still remaining on your credit report.

Bankruptcy

Month, Date, Year
Name of Account Holder
Address
City, State, Zip
RE: Account #

Dear: Manager,

I had an account with your company which unfortunately due to a situation beyond my control, I was unable to meet my debt obligations due to my company downsizing and cutting my work hours to less than half. This left me no choice but to file bankruptcy.

Now that I have finished filing I would like you to remove this account from any and all bureaus you report to as this is already reflecting in bankruptcy. It is also reflecting again as derogatory, which is incorrect, as this is now closed by the bankruptcy court.

Please let me know of your decision in this matter.

Thank you,
Your Name
Address
City, State, Zip

> *Cease and Desist to use when the account has been filed in a Bankruptcy and the creditor is still trying to collect the debt.*

CEASE AND DESIST

Name of Collection Company
Address
City, State Zip
Month, Date, Year

Re: Account #Numbers Company: Original Company

To Whom It May Concern:

According to the Fair Debt Collection Practices Act, Section 805, I have the right to demand that you cease and desist all further communication with me. I hereby give official notice to you and your firm to stop your attempts to contact me in my manner regarding the above debt.

If you continue to contact or attempt to contact me I will be forced to take legal action against you

Do not report any erroneous information to the credit bureaus regarding this debt, if you have I demand you remove it from my credit reports from any and all bureaus to whom you report to immediately or I will take further legal action for violations of the Fair Credit Reporting Act.

A copy of this letter will also be sent to the Federal Trade Commission, State Attorney General and the Better Business Bureau if you do not immediately honor this formal cease and desist request.

Your immediate attention to this matter will be greatly appreciated.

This account was filed in my Chapter 7 Bankruptcy and has been dismissed.

Sincerely,
You're Name
Address
City, State, Zip

> *Use this document if the account is in bankruptcy, but not yet listed on your credit report. You might have to send the creditor a copy of your dismissal papers showing your account in the list of creditors that were filed on, in doing this you are trying to keep this account from being placed on your credit reports. It will keep you from having to dispute this account, therefore, prolonging your credit cleanup efforts.*

Name of Creditor
Address
City, State and Zip
Month Date, Year
Re: Account # Number

To Whom It May Concern:

After ordering my credit report from the credit bureaus it has come to my attention that an account with your company is reporting an account in error.

This account has been closed when it was filed in my Chapter _____ bankruptcy.

Please update your records and correct this error with all credit bureaus that you report to. Please remove this as an individual account as it is now grouped within the bankruptcy.

Please send me confirmation as to this letter sent to you.

Thank you,
You're Name
Address
City, State, Zip

Use this document to dispute the accounts that are not yours with each credit bureau. Most people use this when disputing all accounts that were listed in the bankruptcy after the 24 month period.

Credit Bureau Name
Address
City, State & Zip

_____, 200__

To Whom It May Concern:

After having my credit ran while attempting to purchase a home it has come to my attention that accounts that are not mine are reporting on my report. Please remove these accounts listed below:

- List each account in this box that was inclued in your bankruptcy

Thank You,
Your name
Address
City, State, Zip
Social Security Number: _____ - _____ - _____
Date of Birth: _____ - _____ - _____

CHAPTER 3

Collections

COLLECTION ACCOUNTS LISTED WITH A COLLECTION AGENCY

If you have any accounts that have been sent by your original creditor to a collection agency for collecting the debt, then you have legal options.

In this chapter, you will have the option to use a variety of documents to resolve this issue that are provided at the end of this chapter.

It is very important to understand how to use these documents and in what order to mail them.

Remember, you only get one chance to get the collection companies to comply with the legal document you will be sending them.

If you send one document and find you have received no results, don't become discouraged. You will notice there is another document you can send them to hopefully see the results you are looking for.

If, at anytime you have an issue or a question about collection companies; you can write or call the Federal Trade Commission at:

FTC-CRC
Washington, DC 20580
877.FTC.HELP (4357)

Or you can look up on the Web, the laws for the Fair Debt Collection Practices Act at www.ftc.gov

It will take time to research and write letters, but it is well worth it; especially, when you will be seeing great results.

What Collection Agencies Can and Cannot Do

Debt collectors, also known as collection agencies, are *not allowed to charge interest without permission from the debtor (meaning you)*. With this information you will understand the right document to use when you receive a letter from a collection agency and notice the charges listed on the billing statement which includes interest from the collection agency along with the balance of the original creditor.

A collection account can legally remain on your credit report indefinately; however, there is no law stating it has to remain and cannot be removed before this time. *It is not against the law to remove an account earlier.*

You can check for the statute of limitation for a debt being able to be collected. Most states will not allow a debt to be collected after a certain time frame, even though credit reports may keep it reporting on your report for a period of seven years or longer. *This is only if you don't do anything to remove it earlier.*

See the statute of limitations following this chapter.

The Seven-year Rule

The account can remain on your credit report for seven years from the date the last payment was received by the original creditor.

Let me make this perfectly clear:

The account can remain seven years from the date of the last payment received by only the original creditor.

The Seven-year Rule does not include collection agencies, whose timelines do not count with credit bureaus.

For instance, if you pay off a collection account, the item *will not* be removed from the credit reports. It will simply be marked as "Paid."

Basically, collection agencies have no legal rights to be included on a credit report. You signed the contract with your original creditor—not a collection agency. You did not give the collection agency your social security number, which is detailed in the following section about social security number not being allowed to be sold.

As you will note from the document listed next from the Fair Credit

Reporting Act what the Seven-year Rule is. Understanding this law will help you to understand which document you will need to send to the original creditor who is trying to collect a debt you once owed with its company. With these guidelines, you will know if this debt is still collectable by the original creditor or if the debt is past the Seven-year Rule and now uncollectable.

According to the Fair Credit Reporting Act 605 (U.S.C.1681c).

§ 605. Requirements relating to information contained in consumer reports [15 U.S.C. § 1681c]

(a) Information excluded from consumer reports. Except as authorized under subsection (b) of this section, no consumer reporting agency may make any consumer report containing any of the following items of information:

(1) Cases under title 11 [United States Code] or under the Bankruptcy Act that, from the date of entry of the order for relief or the date of adjudication, as the case may be, antedate the report by more than 10 years.

(2) Civil suits, civil judgments, and records of arrest that from date of entry, antedate the report by more than seven years or until the governing statute of limitations has expired, whichever is the longer period.

(3) Paid tax liens which, from date of payment, antedate the report by more than seven years.

(4) Accounts placed for collection or charged to profit and loss which antedate the report by more than seven years.[1]

(5) Any other adverse item of information, other than records of convictions of crimes which antedates the report by more than seven years.[1]

    (b) Exempted cases. The provisions of subsection (a) of this section are not applicable in the case of any consumer credit report to be used in connection with

(1) a credit transaction involving, or which may reasonably be expected to involve, a principal amount of $150,000 or more;

(2) the underwriting of life insurance involving, or which may reasonably be expected to involve, a face amount of $150,000 or more; or

(3) the employment of any individual at an annual salary which equals, or which may reasonably be expected to equal $75,000, or more.

    (c) Running of reporting period.

(1) In general. The 7-year period referred to in paragraphs (4) and (5) ** of subsection (a) shall begin, with respect to any delinquent account that is placed for collection (internally or by referral to a third party, whichever is earlier), charged to profit and loss, or subjected to any similar action, upon the expiration of the 180-day period beginning on the date of the commencement of the delinquency which immediately preceded the collection activity, charge to profit and loss, or similar action.

(2) Effective date. Paragraph (1) shall apply only to items of information added to the file of a consumer on or after the date that is 455 days after the date of enactment of the Consumer Credit Reporting Reform Act of 1996.

For Example:

You made a payment to AAA Loan Company and then lost your job and were unable to make the February payment.

Your account becomes seven months behind and AAA Loan Company sells your account to BBB Collection Agency to collect the balance of the loan you owed when you stopped making your payments.

You receive a collection notice from BBB Collection Agency stating it is the account holder of your AAA Loan Company account—the original creditor.

You see that the BBB Collection Agency balance for your loan from AAA Loan Company is not the same amount you show in your account statements. BBB Collection Company is charging you the amount for the original debt balance as well as interest at a rate that BBB Collection Agency decides it should charge.

The collection company also will add on charges for collecting the debt in the amount of $ 50-$5,000. There unfortunately is no set amount.

What is a Collection Agency

A collection agency is a business that pursues payments on debts owed by individuals or businesses. Most collection agencies operate as agents of creditors and collect debts for a fee or percentage of the total amount owed. Some agencies, sometimes referred to as "debt buyers," purchase debts from creditors for a fraction of the value of the debt and pursue the debtor for the full balance.

Creditors typically send debts to a collection agency in order to remove them from their accounts receivable records; the difference between the amount collected and the full value of the debt is then written off as a loss.

In many countries, collection agencies are governed by laws that prohibit certain abusive practices. Failure to adhere to such laws may result in lawsuits or government regulatory actions.

When a debt is paid to a collection agency, by the original creditor, the money is theirs to keep. Not one penny is forwarded to your original creditor, because they have already been paid by the collection agency. (Debt collectors for the collection agencies work on commission and this is why they are highly motivated to convince debtors to pay the debt, often to the point that they sound threatening over the phone or by mail.)

The original creditor will mark your credit bureau as "sold to another lender" or "transferred to another lender." Sometimes, they will mark it as, "charged off," when in fact, the account was sold.

What is Sale of Debt

The Sale of Debt or debt buying industry has developed principally in the United States and the debt purchase market is burgeoning in the UK, Europe and Asia.

It allows creditors to generate immediate revenue from their accounts receivables, save infrastructure costs associated with managing collection agencies, and avoid the possible legal liability and public relations risks associated with debt collection.

The Fair Debt Collection Practices Act

What The Fair Debt Collection Practices Act (FDCPA) law states regarding adding interest from the collection agency:

Congress enacted the FDCPA in 1977. It prohibits several of these techniques, including, for example, disclosing consumers' debt to most third parties, which includes a collection agency, without the consumer's consent—meaning you. Debt collectors may not add charges to the debt unless you have agreed to them.

Also FDCPA is the primary United States Federal law governing debt collection practices. The FDCPA allows aggrieved consumers to file private lawsuits against a collection agency that violates the Act. Alternately, the Federal Trade Commission or the state attorney general may take action against a noncompliant collection agency, including issuing fines, ordering damages, restricting its operations or even closing it down.

Following are letters I received from the Federal Trade Commission regarding this issue. Please read through them.

- The first letter is how to contact them if you should have any questions.

- The second letter, dated Aug. 6, 2004, says a debt collector cannot charge interest without your permission and it details how to legally stop collection agencies from contacting you again.

When you have knowledge and the law behind you, you will see you are able to do this on your own and see great results.

Consumer Response Center

UNITED STATES OF AMERICA
FEDERAL TRADE COMMISSION
WASHINGTON, D.C. 20580

November 05, 2003

Sherry Vanapool
1711 Duarte Dr.
Henderson, NV 89014

Re: FTC Ref. No. 3500171

Dear Sherry Vanapool:

Thank you for contacting us. The information you requested is enclosed. For your future needs, you may also want to visit our web page at WWW.FTC.GOV. There you will find many consumer education brochures, as well as our press releases and a host of other important consumer information. You also can submit a complaint directly to us using our new electronic complaint form.

You can always call us toll-free at 1-877-FTC-HELP [1-877-382-4357], or write to:

FTC-CRC
Washington, DC 20580

For one stop access to federal consumer information, check out the U.S. Consumer Gateway web page. Located at WWW.CONSUMER.GOV, the U.S. Consumer Gateway offers information from federal agencies arranged by subject. The site allows consumers to locate and link to appropriate information and websites quickly and easily, including the FTC's new Identity Theft Clearinghouse site at WWW.CONSUMER.GOV/IDTHEFT.

And, finally, if you have a concern about identity theft, you can submit an Identity Theft complaint online or call the toll-free Identity Theft Hotline: 1-877-IDTHEFT (1-877-438-4338), or write to: Identity Theft Clearinghouse, Federal Trade Commission, Washington DC 20580.

We appreciate any comments or suggestions you may have about our service; please mail such feedback to us at the address above. Once again, thank you for contacting us.

Sincerely,

Consumer Response Center

Enclosures:
1. Best Sellers for Consumers & Businesses (GEN-01)

UNITED STATES OF AMERICA
FEDERAL TRADE COMMISSION
WASHINGTON, D.C. 20580

Consumer Response Center

August 06, 2004

Sherri Vanderpool
1711 Duarte Dr
Henderson, NV 89014

Re: FTC Ref. No. 4797109

Dear Ms. Sherri Vanderpool:

    Thank you for your correspondence regarding debt collection practices. The Federal Trade Commission enforces the Fair Debt Collection Practices Act ("FDCPA" or "Act"), which prohibits unfair, deceptive and abusive debt collection practices by collection agencies and other third-party debt collectors. It also gives you certain rights when you are being treated improperly by a debt collector. Although the FTC staff is not in a position to intervene on your behalf in resolving your problem, we would like to outline some of the provisions of the Act for you and explain how you can use it to avoid further distress. We note at the outset, however, that the Act generally does not cover either the collection of commercial debts or the collection activities of the party to whom you allegedly owe your debt (the creditor) so long as the creditor is collecting in its own name. The Act applies only to third-party debt collectors collecting consumer debts.

    Congress enacted the FDCPA in 1977 in response to mounting evidence of the use of improper debt collection techniques in the marketplace. The Act prohibits several of these techniques, including, for example, disclosing consumers' debts to most third parties without the consumers' consent. It also forbids false threats to coerce payment (such as threats of suit or other actions when they probably will never occur) and any sort of oral harassment (such as threats of violence, profanity, and continuous calls) over the telephone. No calls may be made very early in the morning or late at night, calls to a consumer at work are restricted, and debt collectors may not add charges to the debt unless the consumer has agreed to them or they are permitted by state law. Finally, a debt collector may not sue a consumer outside the district (1) of the consumer's residence or (2) where the contract creating the debt was signed.

    If you believe that you do not owe the debt, you may file a dispute with the debt collector. If you do so in writing within thirty days of the date the collector notifies you of this right, the Act requires the collector to stop all collection efforts until it provides you with written verification of the debt. The Act also specifies that the debt collector inform you of this requirement at the beginning of the collection process. If you were not so informed, the collector violated the law.

    Instead of filing a dispute, you may choose to send them a letter demanding that the debt collector cease all further collection efforts. If you do so in writing, the Act requires that the collector comply with the demand. We suggest that you send the letter by certified mail, return

EXAMPLE OF LETTERS FOR YOUR USE

Included are some examples of letters you can use to send to your collection agencies to get them to stop with all collections. In most circumstances they do comply.

A legal method, which is one of my documents, is that a collection company and the original creditor cannot buy or sell a person's social security number. Also, a collection agency cannot sell the account that it was not able to collect on to another collection agency. Which means: An original creditor sells the delinquent account to a collection agency... *or* the collection agency approaches the original creditor and asks if it can purchase the account for so much on a dollar. This is the same with a collection agency selling to another collection agency. It happens every day.

The following is information that states this is illegal.

The Social Security Number Privacy Act (S-324) taken from the Internet Site of the Social Security Administration

Bill Prohibits Sale or Purchase of SS Numbers

Paul M. Alberta

Online Exclusive, Feb 21, 2001

Senator Richard Shelby (R-AL) has sponsored a bill prohibiting financial institutions from buying or selling Social Security numbers.

The Social Security Number Privacy Act (S-324) plugs a loop hole in the 2-year-old Financial Services Modernization Act (FSMA) that revised the nation's financial service's industry.

Under the FSMA financial service firms are permitted to merge and share customer information to offer competing products and services but are prohibited from sharing confidential customer data with affiliated and unaffiliated third parties without permission.

While financial institutions could sell a vast amount of information about their customers to third parties, Shelby said, there was nothing in the FSMA that prohibited them "from buying and selling individual Social Security Numbers."

Noting that financial institutions have used Social Security Numbers as personal identifiers, he added that the buying and selling of them "facilitates criminal activity and can result in a significant invasion of individual privacy."

The legislation would classify individual Social Security Numbers as "nonpublic personal information" under the FSMA, meaning that while they could not be sold, a financial institution could share them with any of their affiliates.

Shelby's bill would also require various federal regulating agencies, including both the Federal Reserve Board and the Federal Trade Commission, to develop stiff new rules enforcing restrictions on the use of Social Security Numbers.

It is the second major bill relating to the use of individual Social Security Numbers to be introduced so far this year. Last month, Rep.

Ron Paul introduced the Identity Theft Protection Act (HR-220), which would prohibit various local, state and federal agencies from using Social Security Numbers as a personal identifier or disclosing them to anyone, including marketers.

They only could be used by the Social Security Administration in connection with its benefits programs and by the Internal Revenue Service for tax purposes.

(Below taken from <u>Gramm-Leach-Bliley Act</u> on the Internet)

Social Security Number Privacy Act of 2001 (Introduced in Senate)

S 324 IS

107th CONGRESS

1st Session

S. 324

To amend the Gramm-Leach-Bliley Act, to prohibit the sale and purchase of the social security number of an individual by financial institutions, to include social security numbers in the definition of nonpublic personal information, and for other purposes.

In The Senate Of The United States

February 14, 2001

Mr. SHELBY introduced the following bill; which was read twice and referred to the Committee on Banking, Housing, and Urban Affairs

A BILL

To amend the Gramm-Leach-Bliley Act, to prohibit the sale and purchase of the social security number of an individual by financial institutions, to include social security numbers in the definition of nonpublic personal information, and for other purposes.

Be it enacted by the Senate and House of Representatives of the United States of America in Congress assembled,

SECTION 1. SHORT TITLE.

This Act may be cited as the 'Social Security Number Privacy Act of 2001'.

SEC. 2. AMENDMENTS RESTRICTING THE SALE AND PURCHASE OF SOCIAL SECURITY NUMBERS.

(a) IN GENERAL- Section 502 of the Gramm-Leach-Bliley Act (15 U.S.C. 6802) is amended by adding at the end the following:

(f) REGULATION OF THE SALE AND PURCHASE OF SOCIAL SECURITY NUMBERS AND SOCIAL SECURITY ACCOUNT NUMBERS-

(1) PROHIBITION- Notwithstanding any other provision of this title, no financial institution may sell or purchase a social security number or a social security account number in a manner that violates a regulation promulgated by the Federal functional regulators under paragraph (2).

(2) REGULATIONS-

(A) IN GENERAL- Not later than 6 months after the date of enactment of the Social Security Number Privacy Act of 2001, the Federal functional regulators shall promulgate regulations restricting the sale and purchase of social security numbers and social security account numbers by financial institutions.

Privacy

The Act includes provisions providing consumers with certain protections with respect to the transfer and use of their "nonpublic" personal information by financial institutions, including giving consumers the option to "opt out" of having their personal financial information shared with nonaffiliated third parties, subject to certain exceptions.

Congress passed the Financial Services Modernization Act of 1999 on November 4, 1999.

In Conclusion

You do have the law on your side. By reading this book, you are now aware of your options to correcting the negative entries on your credit reports for all credit bureaus.

- Don't get discouraged when working to get collection accounts completely deleted from your reports. This is a process and does take time, so be patient. You will not regret your decision to attempt to improve your credit file by doing this on your own.

- It is well worth your efforts to remove the collection accounts without your having to pay the debt because your original creditor has already closed your account and written it off.

- Some collection accounts were sold from the original creditor even though the accounts were in fact paid. It is a good suggestion to keep good clear records for at least seven years. When you paid off an account, keep the receipt proving your payment.

- If an insurance company paid on a medical debt that was billed to the hospital, it is a very good idea to keep your receipt as most insurance companies do pay the medical bill, but the medical facility doesn't log the payment made to them.

- The medical facility may bill you, hoping to receive payment again for the same debt, or someone who works in the billing office doesn't log the payment received from the insurance company. This is the most common type of collection account.

So, remember, keeping good records and paid receipts will give you what you need to prove your account history and payment record so you won't have to worry that accounts listed on your credit reports will not be able to be corrected.

Website to see the 7 year rule.

http://www.ftc.gov/os/statutes/031224fcra.pdf

As you will note in the FTC document that a collection company doesn't have many rights to your account, all you need to do is send a collection company a "Cease and Desist" document as you would rather work with your original creditor.

You will find that even though you send out this Cease and Desist document to each collection company the original creditor has already closed the account. The original creditor will no longer talk to you about the account as it is now closed by either selling the account to the collection company, or the original creditor charging the account off.

This is to your advantage because usually in most circumstances the original creditor will remove the account from the credit report all together

Now by sending the Cease and Desist document to the collection companies you will be getting this account completely deleted from your reports without having to pay your debt in most situations. It is not 100% guaranteed but it is a start to getting the account deleted permanently

Take a look at the different types of Cease and Desist documents that are listed at the end of this chapter. There is a brief description as to what document to use for the different types of accounts you are addressing.

There is a document for to use when two collection companies are trying to collect for the same debt… The original creditor does sometimes sell your account to more than one collection agency. When this happens you will receive billing invoices from each collection agency letting you know they now are the company in charge of collecting for your account. Don't let this confuse you with the right document to send out, as the legal documents I have given you will help you with this issues and others you might encounter.

> *Cease and Desist letter to use with most all collection agencies*

CEASE AND DESIST

Creditors Name
Address
City, State, Zip
Month, Date, Year

Re: Account # Number   Company: Original Creditor

To Whom It May Concern:

According to the Fair Debt Collection Practices Act, Section 805, I have the right to demand that you cease and desist all further communication with me. I hereby give official notice to you and your firm to stop your attempts to contact me in my manner regarding the above debt.

If you continue to contact or attempt to contact me I will be forced to take legal action against you. *I would prefer to resolve this problem with the original company with whom I have contracted, not with you or any other agency.*

Do not report any erroneous information to the credit bureaus regarding this debt, if you have I demand you remove it from my credit reports from any and all bureaus to whom you report to immediately or I will take further legal action for violations of the Fair Credit Reporting Act.

A copy of this letter will also be sent to the Federal Trade Commission, State Attorney General and the Better

Business Bureau if you do not immediately honor this formal cease and desist request.

Your immediate attention to this matter will be greatly appreciated.

According to the Fair Credit Reporting Act 605 (U.S.C. 1681c) The general rule of the 7-year period beginning on the date of the original delinquency of the original creditor. The account you are reporting is at or past the 7-years. Please comply and remove from any and all bureaus that you report to.

Sincerely,
You're Name
Address
City, State, Zip
Social Security # ____ - ____ - ____
Date of Birth: ____ - ____ - ____

> *Cease and desist to use when more than one collection company is collecting for the same debt. If a collection company name for example is: (today's collection) is collecting for "My new furniture" and on your credit report you notice another collection company named: (2nd collection company) is trying to collect for the exact same debt. You will then send this document to each of the collection companies.*

Note: be sure to change the collection company name in the middle of this document. This area is written in red.

DEBT VALIDATION VERIFICATION

,200

Name of Collection Company
Address
City, State Zip
RE: Account # Number   For: Name of Original Creditor

To Whom It May Concern:

I have just received a copy of my credit report and noticed an account from your company on it, please validate this account. According to FCRA §611, part B, subsection (iii) & FDCPA 623 according to Federal standards.

1. Proof that the collection agency was assigned the debt and has the legal authority to collect on behalf of the creditor.

2. Complete payment history.

52 | *"The Legal Method" To Clearing Your Own Credit*

3. Copy of the original signed agreement or application.

Please validate this information and correct it with any credit bureaus to whom you have reported adverse information about my credit rating. If the information cannot be validated, please delete the account from my credit reports and **cease and desist with all collection efforts.**

This account is also listed with: You cannot collect for debt that is being collected by another company.

Please inform me as to the result of your validation within 5 days. Your immediate attention to this matter is appreciated.

Cc: State Attorney's General FDCPA

Sincerely,
You're Name
Address
City, State, Zip

Cease and Desist Validation. This document is used usually the very first time a Cease and Desist is sent out. This is the first one you should use, if you don't get the results you want, and then you can send out a different document to hopefully get the results you are looking for.

DEBT VALIDATION AND VERIFICATION

Month, Date, Year
Collection Company
Address
City, State, Zip
RE: Account #   For: Company their collection for

To Whom It May Concern:

I have just received a copy of my credit report and noticed an account from your company on it. Please validate this account. According to FCRA §611, part B, subsection (iii) & FDCPA 623 according to Federal standards.

1. Proof that the collection agency was assigned the debt and has the legal authority to collect on behalf of the creditor.
2. Complete payment history.
3. Copy of the original signed agreement or application.

Please validate this information and correct it with any credit bureaus to whom you have reported adverse information about my credit rating. If the information cannot be validated, please delete the account from my credit reports and **cease and desist with all collection efforts.**

Please inform me as to the result of your validation within 5 days. Your immediate attention to this matter is appreciated.

Cc: State Attorney's General
FDCPA

Sincerely,
You're Name
Address
City, State, Zip

> Collection Company and the original creditor showing the same account on the credit reports. Usually only one account can be listed at a time. Not 2 different names with the same account numbers. This will make your credit report, report the same account twice.

Name of creditor
Address
City, State Zip
Month date, 2005

To: Credit Manager,

Enclosed is a copy of a bill from your company along with a bill from a collection agency showing the same company as yours with the same account number # 123456. Both are reflecting on my credit reports.

To the best of my knowledge I wasn't aware of having an open account with your company. I would like to honor my debt if this is in fact mine.

Please send me a contract showing me that I signed for merchandise. After receiving this I will be happy to settle this account with you. Please correct this with Name the creditor. I will only settle this account with you directly if I do in fact owe this debt.

Please send me the proper documents proving this account.

Thank you,
Your name
Address
City, State Zip

This is a letter you will send to a collection company after paying off the original creditor. Just fill in the highlighted areas such as: date, address, account number, what account it is for etc.

Date, Month, Year
Collection Company
Address
City, State, Zip
Regarding Account #   For:

To Whom It May Concern:

It has been brought to my attention that you feel I owed you a financial obligation for a bill that belonged to   .

I never contracted with your company, I however was seen and had services provided from   , which entitles them to receive payment for their services.

I never contracted or signed a contract agreeing to pay your company any fees.

Please delete your account from any and all credit reporting agencies you report to. I do not give you authorization to slander my credit rating.

A copy of this letter will be sent to agencies listed below, if you fail to comply with my request:

   * FTC

* FDCPA

* States Attorney General

Please send me confirmation you will comply.

Thank you,
You're Name
Address
City, State, Zip

> *Send this document to the original creditor asking them to remove the account from the collection agency. You have no knowledge of this account. It is not yours. Just fill in the shaded areas.*

Month Date, 2007
Original creditors name
Address
City, State, Zip

To Whom It May Concern:

I just recently noticed an account from your company is reflecting on my credit report. Would you please correct this mistake, as I don't believe I owe any money to   .

The account number, which is showing, is: #   … The balance is $ since   of   .

It is showing as being placed with   .

Please let me know of your findings. Please remove this account from

Thank you,
You're Name
Address
City, state, Zip

CHAPTER 4

Statute of Limitations

In Chapter 3, I discussed the rights of the Statute of Limitations and what this means to you regarding options you have in clearing up your credit accounts. Below, you will see what the definition means so you will be able to understand what type of account you will be working on.

STATUTE OF LIMITATIONS

Statute of Limitations fixes a definite period of time within which a civil legal action or a criminal prosecution must be commenced. A person, such as a plaintiff who has a cause of action to sue a person, loses the right of action if he/she fails to institute legal proceedings within the time limit set by their state for that particular legal action.

Another way to describe the Statute of limitations is that a timeline of collecting a debt has expired, so it is not a collectable debt any longer.

CONTRACTS

There are many types of contracts in society that are legal and binding in a court of law. They are under a timeline or statute of limitation as to what timeframe each type of contract is collectable or uncollectable. In order to understand which type of contract you have, I have listed the most common.

Oral Contract: You have agreed to pay money lent under a verbal agreement with no written contract. Basically, you agree and then shake hands. Remember that a verbal contract is legal, but much tougher to prove in court.

Written Contract: You have agreed to pay back a loan based on written terms and a signed contract.

Promissory Note: This is similar to a written contract; however, a promissory note is a written contract that schedules payments and spells out the interest on the loan. An example of a promissory note is a mortgage or car loan.

Open Ended Accounts: These are revolving accounts such as credit cards.

The "Statute of Limitations" is Vital in the World of Credit

Each day, ordinary people pay off collection accounts and charge-offs that they did not have to pay because the statute of limitations had already expired. They pay them because the accounts continue to appear on their credit reports. The consumer is under the impression that the credit bureaus are reporting accurately—*only because they are not aware of their rights.*

With the payoff to the collection account, the negative reporting is removed from a credit file. Yet, the consumer needed only to have said to the collector: "I have an absolute defense: the statute of limitations has expired."

The debt was accumulated by you, but if the statute of limitations in force has expired, and the creditor tries to force you to pay the debt, you have the right to not fulfill the promise of the debt through the statute of limitations.

1. As far as the credit bureaus are concerned, the statute of limitations does not cause your debt to go away after it expires.

2. The statute of limitations causes the law to be on your side if this account was to be filed in court after the statute of limitations expires—which allows the debt to be cancelled.

3. If the statute of limitations has expired, it doesn't mean it will automatically come off your credit report. But it is an opportunity to get this account deleted from your credit report the legal way.

4. If the creditor files suit, you, the consumer, have an absolute defense. You must offer the new evidence to avoid a judgment if it is filed. The evidence will consist of papers you file to support your claim—which is what this book is all about.

If the creditor sues you, and you do not prove to the court that the statute of limitations expired, you will have a lost lawsuit and a judgment will be placed on your credit reports, causing your credit to be damage further.

Keeping Good Records to Prove Your Statute of Limitations

When you have credit accounts, it is an excellent habit to always keep a copy of the last billing statement. This is important; especially, if your accounts go into the negative status because you are not able to continue to pay on them in a timely fashion.

Keep accurate records when you begin receiving account notices from your creditors informing you that your account has gone into the negative status and are in jeopardy of being charged-off.

1. Scan the notices into your computer and save them on a USB-thumb drive or back up CD.
2. Keep these in a safe place such as a fire-safe box or anywhere you know you will always be able to get to it if needed.
3. Keep these records for at least seven years as this is how long they can remain on your credit reports.
4. It is also a good idea to keep a copy of an old credit report. If

the item is not removed from a current credit report, you will be able to prove when it was first placed on your report.

I once had a client who kept her reports for nine years, (yes, I agree with you, who in their right mind would keep a credit report this long?) But it was a good thing she had kept this report. She actually found that the same accounts were still reporting. They were just being renewed by different debt collectors who were reporting the accounts as new, while the old collection accounts were then reporting to the bureaus as "sold to another lender." This will cause the credit score to be damaged even more than just having the original credit reporting as a charge-off.

Once she proved to the credit bureaus, using copies of these old reports and sent them a copy of her new report, the accounts were deleted by the credit bureau immediately. If this client had not had good records, the accounts might have remained indefinitely.

Your Goal is to Stop Duplicate Reporting

The goal is to remove negative accounts before seven years is up.

From my experience, when an account is sold to a collection company and the debt is not settled, the collection company will then sell the account to another collection company because it wants to recoup its initial investment of purchasing the account from the original creditor.

When the 2nd collection company purchases the account, it will report the account as just going into delinquency. *Meaning the timeframe for this account has begun the seven years once again.*

By keeping good records of when the account originally went into delinquency, you will always be able to prove the exact date of when your delinquency began—along with the name, address and account number of the original creditor to prove your case.

You will find that sometime during the seven years of this account, it will be up to you to prove this. You might have to send a copy of a delinquent account to the credit bureaus themselves to prove the date of the original creditor and when the account first went into delinquency.

Statute of Limitations in Your State

If you are ever sued by a collection agency or from an original creditor, you also have the benefit of the timeframe regarding the statute of limitation for the state you live in.

For instance, for the state of New York, an oral agreement is four years. Which means this is an uncollectable debt after four years. If the creditor sues you in court after four years, you have records to prove the account has been in default for longer than four years, which is in your favor. Therefore, a judgment or wage garnishment will not be granted against you.

For a written contract the statute of limitations is six years. A promissory note, such as a mortgage, is three years. For an open ended account, such as a credit card, it is four years.

It is always good to know what type of legalities will be helpful to help you with creditors. *Don't be bullied into paying a debt that you are no longer legally bound to pay.*

STATUTE OF LIMITATIONS CHART BY STATE

The State Where You Live	Oral Agreements	Written Contract	Promissory Notes (Mortgages)	Open Ended Accounts
	Years	Years	Years	Years
Alabama	6	6	6	3
Alaska	3	3	6	6
Arizona	3	6	4	4
Arkansas	5	5	6	3
California	2	4	4	4
Colorado	6	6	6	6
Connecticut	3	6	6	6
Delaware	3	3	6	3
D.C.	3	3	3	3
Florida	4	5	5	4
Georgia	4	6	6	4
Hawaii	6	6	6	6
Idaho	4	5	10	4
Indiana	5	10	6	5
Illinois	6	10	10	6
Iowa	5	10	10	5
Kansas	3	5	5	3
Kentucky	5	15	15	5
Louisiana	10	10	10	3
Maine	6	6	6	6
Maryland	3	3	6	3
Massachusetts	6	6	6	6

Statute of Limitations

Michigan	6	6	6	6
Minnesota	6	6	6	6
Mississippi	3	3	3	3
Missouri	5	10	10	5
Montana	5	8	8	5
Nebraska	4	5	6	4
Nevada	4	5	6	4
New Hampshire	3	3	6	3
New Jersey	6	6	6	6
New Mexico	4	6	6	4
New York	6	6	6	6
North Carolina	6	6	6	6
North Dakota	6	6	6	6
Ohio	6	15	15	0
Oklahoma	3	5	5	3
Oregon	6	6	6	6
Pennsylvania	4	6	4	6
Rhode Island	15	15	10	10
South Carolina	3	3	3	3
South Dakota	6	6	6	6
Tennessee	6	6	6	6
Texas	4	4	4	4
Utah	4	6	6	4
Vermont	6	6	5	6
Virginia	3	5	6	3

Washington	3	6	6	3
Wisconsin	5	10	6	5
West Virginia	6	6	10	6
Wyoming	8	10	10	8

CHAPTER 5

Asking for Forgiveness or Verification from your Creditors

HOW TO ASK FORGIVENESS OR VERIFICATION FOR AN ACCOUNT

Have you ever wondered if a debt that you paid late could ever be corrected or the late payment could be forgiven or completely "deleted" from your credit reports by the account holder (creditor)?

Meaning, the account holders change your credit reports with the three credit bureaus, Equifax, Experian and Trans Union.

Most Americans aren't aware that a late payment can, in fact, be updated to reflect "paid, never late" by the original creditor as they choose to "forgive the late payment."

It takes a simple request in writing using the legal forms I have included in this chapter.

Once you have mailed the legal form to each account holder that is reporting late payments on your reports, you will be mailed an updated letter that states it your original creditor will be removing the late payments and will, in fact, be notifying all credit bureaus to whom they report.

NOTE: It is a good idea to always keep records of all documents you receive. This is so that a particular company that has already removed its late payment history from your file cannot change its mind and put it back on. (Sometimes, if a company's manager has decided to leave a company, a new manager might see the payment history and have the late payments added to your report.)

With good records, this will not be allowed to happen, as the company has already agreed to remove the late payments in writing.

Enhancing Your Credit Score

Accounts can remain on your reports for a term of seven years. It is a good idea to remove these negative reporting accounts because it will keep your credit score lowered.

The following are areas to ask for forgiveness, such as:

- Forgiveness of the debt completely.
- Forgiveness of a late payment on opened account.
- Forgiveness of late payment on accounts that are already paid in full.

Forgiveness of Debt Document

Use this document after an account is paid in full and it has not reported to the credit bureaus as paid in full. The document will request they remove this account completely from your credit file. You will only want to do this if the account had a very low credit limit ($500 and lower).

Forgiveness of Late Payment on an Open Account Document

In this document, you are requesting all late payments on this account to be forgiven and updated to reflect that you have never paid late. You will be amazed at how willing people are to help and make the necessary changes when you ask. By removing the late payments, while keeping the account with a prior credit history on your reports, this will help to increase your credit score.

Forgiveness of a Late Payment on a Paid Off Account Document

You will use this document to request the creditor forgive you for paying the account late. This is used only for a paid off account that will give you a good credit rating because the amount of credit line was good.

Verification of a Debt

When you have a creditor that is stating on your reports that you have an account with them, but to your recollection you don't remember opening this account you have a right to request in writing for them to verify this debt.

Simply mail them in a Verification of Debt form. If the debt is yours this company will then mail you the documentation proving this debt to be yours, usually by sending you a contract with your signature on it.

If this debt is not found by this company, they will mail you a letter stating this account was not found.

You can use this letter to mail to the credit bureaus that are reporting this account on your reports requesting them to remove the account.

> F.O.D... Forgiveness of Debt. Just fill in the shaded area with the correct information. This document is used after an account is paid in full and it is not reporting to the credit bureaus as paid in full. It is also requesting they remove this account completely from your credit file. You will only want to do this if the account had a very low credit limit ($500.00 and lower). Remember you are working to build your credit file. Then dispute this account with the credit bureaus as "Not Mine".

_____, 200_

Name of Creditor
Address
City, State, Zip
Re: Account number

My account with you is current paid in full. Please notify all credit bureaus you report to regarding this. Also would you please change my file to reflect paid in full and satisfactory? Please remove all derogatory information regarding this account as I honored my debt.

Please send my confirmation on your decision as to my request.

Thank you,
You're Name
Address
City, State, Zip

F.O.L, ALSO KNOWN AS: FORGIVENESS OF LATE PAYMENT.

> *In this document you are requesting all Lates paid on this account to be forgiven and updated to reflect that you have never paid late. You will be amazed at how well people are willing to help and make the necessary changes when you ask. Just fill in the shaded areas. Then you will dispute this account with the credit bureaus so it will be updated and deleted.*

FORGIVENESS OF LATE

, 200

Name of Creditor

Address

City, State, Zip

RE: Account

To Whom It May Concern:

There is an account from your company reporting on my credit report that, states that I have paid my account late. Please verify the dates this happened or please change the status of this account and payment history to reflect paid on time, never late.

I have no knowledge of this being paid late.

If I did pay this account late it was not intentional, due to reasons beyond my control it could not be helped.

Please consider changing this status of my account to paid as agreed with no late.

Please notify me as to your decision.

Thank you,
You're Name
Address
City, State, Zip

> *F.O.L Paid off account. You will use this document to request the creditor forgive you for paying the account late. This is used only for a paid off account that will give you a good credit rating because the amount of credit line was good. Just fill in the shaded areas. Then dispute this account as "Never Late" with the credit bureaus.*

FORGIVENESS OF LATE

, 2007

Creditors Name
Address
City, State, Zip
RE: Account

To Whom It May Concern:

There is an account from your company reporting on my credit report that, states that I have paid my account late. Please verify the dates this happened or please change the status of this account and payment history to reflect paid on time, never late.

This account is paid and is now closed.

I have no knowledge of this being paid late.

If I did pay this account late it was not intentional, due to reasons beyond my control it could not be helped.

Please consider changing this status of my account to paid as agreed with no late.

Please notify me as to your decision.

Thank you,
You're Name
Address
City, State, Zip

CHAPTER 6

Student Loans

THE STUDENT LOAN HOOK

Many people who have sought an education have most likely taken out a student loan.

There you were in the counselor's office who told you that you *could afford* to go to school because the government offers very affordable student loans. It does not have to be paid back until long after you finish school. By that time, you will have landed a wonderful job that pays you more income that you ever thought you would be able to make.

You also were told that the interest is very low.

The Truth

You finish school and find out that you actually owe thousands of dollars to the government for student loans. *The interest has been accumulating during the years you were in school, causing the final results to be as follows:*

For every $100 you pay back for your student loan, only $10 goes towards the principle. This is just an example and rates may vary, depending on your loan.

What you need to know is that if you qualify, there are ways to have a student loan canceled.

Canceling a Student Loan

Depending on the type of loan you have and when you obtained it, you may be able to cancel your loan under one of the following circumstances:

- You become totally and permanently disabled.
- The former student has died.
- You serve in the U.S. military.
- You're a full-time elementary or secondary school teacher in a designated area serving low-income students.
- You're a full-time teacher of children with disabilities in a public or other nonprofit elementary or secondary school.
- You're a full-time professional provider of early intervention services for the disabled.

- You're a full-time professional provider of early intervention services for the disabled.

- You're a full-time teacher of math, science, foreign languages, bilingual education or other fields designated as teacher-shortage areas.

- You're a full-time employee of a public or nonprofit agency providing services to low-income, high-risk children and their families.

- You're a full-time nurse or medical technician.

- You're a full-time law enforcement or corrections officer.

- You're a full-time staff member in a Head Start program.

- You're a Peace Corps or VISTA Volunteer.

- Your school closed before you could complete your program of study.

- Your school falsely certified that you were eligible for a student loan.

To cancel a student loan—or to determine if you qualify for cancellation—call the servicer of your loan or the Department of Education's Debt Collection Services office at 800.621.3115.

Getting Out of Default

School is out. You're excited to finally have your degree in the field you have dreamed of—only to find you are unable to obtain the "job of your dreams." You have had to settle for a normal, typical job that does not pay nearly enough to meet your monthly obligations.

As months go by, you receive notices from the servicer of your student loan, reminding you that a payment is due and to let you know that you are in default. You are warned that if you do not take action to rectify this, you will find the outcome not in your favor. The government has many actions it can legally take against you to recover the funds lent to you in good faith.

According to your written and signed agreement, when you borrowed from the government for a student loan or received a grant, you were aware of the consequences of what can happen to your credit, future income and IRS intervention if you fail to pay it back.

If you feel you are lost and have no where to turn for help, you are not alone. And you have the means to get out of default with the student loans that were offered to you by the government. It has many different programs to help you make the right choice for your budget.

STEPS TO RECTIFY A DEFAULT

- When you make six consecutive monthly payments to your lender, this will allow you to regain trust financially and bring you out of default sufficiently enough to be eligible for a new student loan if you want to return to school to complete your education.

- Once you make 12 consecutive payments, the agency holding your loan can sell it to a company that handles payments and collections of student loans, as well as remove the default notification from your credit reports.

- You are now eligible for a *deferment* or *forbearance*, due to financial hardship or other hardships.

A Deferment

With a deferment, the lender gives you a form to fill out with a few questions. As soon as you fill it out and send it back to them, your payments will delay or be postponed until you are able to pay them without a financial hardship. The deferment does not accrue interest because it will be frozen. Therefore, no additional amount will be added to your loan.

Additionally, depending on your lender, you may need to extend this deferment every 6 or 12 months. You will need to keep a record of when it expires and make sure that if you would like to extend it, you notify your lender in a timely manner. Generally, they will extend the loan so you will not be in jeopardy of any further hardship.

A Forbearance

A forbearance is almost the same as a deferment, *except the interest accrual process still continues*. This means that any unpaid interest that accrues and isn't paid off within the period of the forbearance is capitalized. This means the principle will increase in order to allow for this interest to be added.

Why and How to Correct Student Loan Issues on Your Credit File

You will have peace of mind after doing whatever you can to rectify your situation to get out of default.

- If do nothing to rectify this debt, the government has the right to put a wage garnishment against you with your employer until the debt is paid in full.

- The government can also attach all IRS refunds until the debt is paid in full.

- During this process, you also will be responsible to pay penalties and interest of the unpaid amount.

So, contact the provider that holds your student loan to let them know you are interested in working with them to get out of default.

Use this document to cancel your student loan.

                        , 200

Name of Lender
Address
City, State, Zip

To Whom It May Concern:

I currently am repaying a student loan with your company. I understand certain student loans are forgiven depending on the graduate field.

Enclosed are documents which show my certain field of employment and school along with the information regarding student loans.

If this loan can be forgiven under the guidelines of the Education Loan Program, please contact me with what it is I will need to do next.

I am requesting this loan be forgiven.

Sincerely,
You're Name
Address
City, State, Zip

F.O.L Student Loans.

███████ ███████, 2007 ███████

Loan Company
Address
City, State, Zip
RE: Account #

To: Account Specialist,

Thank you for your quick response. I do understand the negatives on this account are not the fault of ███████ and you say this late will remain on my credit report, can you please tell me how long this will remain?

I do understand you can make the decision to remove it earlier than normal. There is no legal document stating exactly how long this will remain on my credit report. I am asking you to forgive this late as this was not intentional. I have always valued my good credit and have not defaulted on my loan with your good company. Would you please reconsider removing this late? I could understand if I was late many times, therefore this would be my fault and done carelessly. Yes, this late was an error on my part, I am very sorry for this; please consider removing this earlier than the normal amount of time.

Sincerely,
You're Name
Address
City, State, Zip

CHAPTER 7

Breaking a Lease Auto, Home or Apartment

BREAK A LEASE? IMPOSSIBLE, YOU SAY

You are thinking it is not possible to break a lease, but with the right document and knowledge, it is possible.

In this chapter you will understand that it is possible to cancel an auto, home or apartment lease simply with the use of each document I have provided at the end of this chapter. It doesn't matter what type of lease you have: It is possible, by law, to legally cancel any type of lease.

Car Lease

When you visit an auto dealership, the salesperson wants to sell you a car—and it doesn't matter if it is a sale or a lease.

In today's market, a lease seems to be a better financial option. You won't lose car value or the depreciation of the vehicle during a trade in. You can trade in your vehicle for a brand new one once the lease you signed and agreed to is up.

But what they don't tell you is this: If you need to turn in the vehicle early, you will have a large penalty to pay. Most people cannot afford the penalty or the damage it can do to their credit report. This makes for the only option to turn the car back in to the dealership and take the negative mark on your credit file.

Now there is hope and help for an early lease turn in.

All you will need to do is the following:

- Fill out the document below for the auto lease and mail it to your account holder.
- Dispute this account with each credit bureau as "not mine."

The key to this document is that the agreement is vague and ambiguous. The definition is that it is too complex to understand or having two or more possible meanings, not clear, indefinite, vague.

If you would like to research more information on this law,

- Go to **www.consumerlaw.org/action_agenda/ e_commerce/interim.shtml**

- Look up code: Federal Consumer Leasing Act (15 U.S.C. §§ 1667-1667e)
- You can also put in a search engine: Federal Consumer Leasing Act and look for the code listed above.

HOME OR APARTMENT LEASE

In today's market, you may be unable to purchase your own home due to your financial situation. It's based on the fact that your credit score is not high enough to secure a home loan through a lender.

Therefore, your only option is to sign a lease agreement with a homeowner directly or a leasing agent or property management company for either a home or an apartment.

As life goes though, events can happen with a job loss or promotion or job offer that asks us to move to another state. Even though you talk to your homeowner or lease management company and explain your current situation, it's very possible that they may not agree to let you out of your lease.

So, you take a hit with a negative mark on your credit file. But, you do not have to settle with having your credit ruined. By using the documents below, you have an option to have your broken lease removed from your credit file.

To break a lease that pertains to your own situation, simply follow the instructions for each document listed at the end of this chapter.

Don't get discouraged. You will be amazed at the results you will be able to obtain on your own—just like the professionals do.

> *Use this document for removing an auto lease, then dispute this account with each credit bureau as "Not Mine".*

Name
Address
City, State Zip
Month Date, 2006
Re: Lease Number: # 123456

To: Accounts Manager

I can no longer make the payments required under my car lease. I would like to schedule a time to bring this vehicle in, preferable date, time.

I have reviewed the clause in my lease agreement which dictates how much I must pay in the event I terminate the lease early. I do not understand the formula. It is ambiguous and complex. Under the federal consumer Leasing Act (15 U.S.C. §§ 1667-1667E), I am not obligated to make additional payments after terminating a lease if the termination formula is unreasonable.

Furthermore, I know that I am entitled to sue you for damages because of your failure to use a reasonable formula. I am willing to waive my right to sue if you will waive your claim for additional payments because of my early termination.

Thank you
Your name
Address
City, State Zip

> *Use this document if you are in an apartment or house lease the same will apply for your lease, Then dispute it with the credit bureaus as, "Not Mine," Or "no knowledge of account"*

Name of Apartment or Lease Manager
Address
City, State or Zip

_____, 200__

Re: Lease or Rental Agreement

To: Apartment Manager / Lease Manager:

I was no longer able to make the payments required under my apartment lease. I have already vacated the premises located at:

Property Address
City, State, Zip

I have reviewed the clause in my lease agreement, which dictates how much I must pay in the event I terminate the lease early. I do not understand the formula. It is vague, ambiguous and complex. Under the federal Consumer Leasing Act (15 U.S.C. §§ 1667-1667e) and The Truth in Lending Act (15 USC 1601 et seq.), I am not obligated to make additional payments after terminating a lease if the termination formula is unreasonable.

Furthermore, I know that I am entitled to sue you for damages because of your failure to use a reasonable formula. I am willing to waive my right to sue if you will waive your claim for additional payments because of my early termination.

Please remove these accounts from any/all bureaus who you report to. Please send me documentation this is being done.

Sincerely,
You're Name
Address
State, Zip

If you would like to research more information on this law please go to: Make sure to look up law 605...

http://www.consumerlaw.org/action_agenda/e_commerce/interim.shtml

Just look up code: Federal Consumer Leasing Act

(15 U.S.C. §§ 1667-1667e)

You can also put in the search engine:

Federal Consumer Leasing Act. Just look for the code listed above.

CHAPTER 8

The IRS

THE INTERNAL REVENUE SERVICE

Creating a debt with the IRS is not an ideal situation for anyone. Most people become nervous and, intentionally or unintentionally, avoid attempting to clear up their tax debt because they have been brainwashed to believe the IRS is always right and they have no other options.

I am here to let you know that this is not true. You do have options and I will show you your options.

THERE IS HOPE

You could spend thousands of dollars paying a taxpayer attorney (if you wish, you can still seek the legal advice from an attorney), but it might behoove you to try to remedy the debt by yourself.

How? There are form letters that can help you with a negotiation to settle your account with the IRS for pennies on the dollar *or have this debt completely deleted from your credit reports as well as closed with the IRS.*

The IRS and collection agencies

Are you aware that the IRS now sends your account to a collection agency if it is in arrears? Meaning, you owed back taxes for some time and the IRS was unable to collect. This could be to your benefit.

In September 2006, the IRS began to outsource the collection of taxpayers' debts to private debt collection agencies.

Opponents noted that the IRS would be handing over personal information to the debt collection agencies, which are being paid between 22% to 24% of the amount collected.

Opponents also were concerned about the agencies being paid on "percentage collected," as it will encourage the collectors to use heavy pressure tactics to collect the maximum amount. An IRS spokesman responded to the critics saying the new system "is a sound, balanced program that respects taxpayers' rights and taxpayer privacy." By the way, other state and local agencies also use private collection agencies.

If your IRS account has been turned over to a collection agency, you have options to correct this situation with the use of the legal documents listed at the end of this chapter.

Refer to Chapter 3 Collection Agencies. The IRS also is required to follow certain guidelines in the Fair Debt Collection Practices Act.

This means you have options to have the account removed from your credit reports.

An Example:

I had a friend who became in debt with the IRS after purchasing a salon: Little did she know that when she purchased this salon, she also purchased the old salon owner's IRS tax debt.

You can imagine how she felt when she realized this situation was not a good one to be in. She found herself in a real dilemma because she was unable to pay the tax.

She hired a tax attorney and found out, after paying a bill of $6,500, that nothing was accomplished.

Instead of continuing to pursue the legal option, she sent a document directly to the IRS, requesting to pay pennies on the dollar. You can imagine how happy and surprised she was when they accepted. She has now cleared the debt that originally was someone else's.

She also disputed the tax liens with each credit bureau as "Not mine." To her surprise, they were totally "deleted."

It Never Hurts to Try

Remember, you don't know what the outcome will be until you do something about it to help yourself.

Never give up! There is always a way to help yourself.

> *Mail this form letter to the I.R.S. get your I.R.S debt settled.*

RE: Docket #
Company Name
Address
City, State Zip

To Whom It May Concern:

It has been brought to my attention I have an outstanding tax lien with your office. I would like clear these tax liens up.

I would like to offer you for:
Docket # _____ $ _____

Would you please accept this amount in order to release these tax liens? This all I am able to afford at this time, I would like to honor these debts but I also need help to do this. I am sorry for the time that has lapsed, as I have not been able to pay these until now. Upon these being paid, is it possible to have these records sealed/closed from the public viewing? If it is I would like to request this at this time.

Please send me confirmation that this is acceptable.

Thank you,
Name
Address
City, State Zip
SS# _____ - _____ - _____
D.O.B. _____ - _____ - _____

CHAPTER 9

Disputes with Credit Bureaus

The following information will assist you in your dealing with the credit bureaus. We will cover:

- Updating vs. Disputing Credit Bureaus Overview
- How to dispute accounts with each credit bureau
- What to do when your credit reports come back from the credit bureaus
- How to get more accounts deleted the second time around
- Once a credit report comes back stating that they verified the accounts
- Inquiry removal

These chapters will guide you through the process, bringing together what you have learned from previous chapters to complete the correction of your credit file.

This is not a difficult process to follow. It is simple with great rewards , resulting in an increase in your credit score so that you may once again have good credit. This will give you great success through low interest in future purchases.

Please be diligent and patient and keep copies of all reports that have been mailed to you. This will allow you to see the results when you compare previous reports.

Updating vs. Disputing Credit Bureaus Overview

Your first step is to "update" the credit bureaus on all the accounts listed on your reports. At this point, you are not yet "disputing." You are fact gathering through legal documents that you have sent to account holders who have been listed on your reports. As a result of your inquiries, you will find that some are reported accurately and some are not. According to the law, original creditors and collection companies, etc. must remove the inaccurate reporting of negative accounts, because you will have brought these accounts to their attention.

The next step is to have as many negative accounts deleted that would otherwise be listed on your reports for seven years and longer. This will be done with a dispute letter.

When you send the credit bureaus the dispute letter, the burden of proof is on the original creditor to prove the validity of the debt in question that is on your report.

With the use of legal documents, the creditor(s) must provide proof that the listed negative account does, in fact, belong to you.

Once you have mailed your legal document to the original creditor, collection company, or any company that is reporting negatively on your credit reports, it is these companies that will remove the account with the credit bureaus.

In other words, when the credit bureaus attempt to verify the accounts during the dispute with the questioned account holders, and the account holders cannot verify the debt, with the credit bureaus, it is then that the credit bureau you are disputing the account with will then delete the account you are disputing.

How to Dispute Accounts with each Credit Bureau

First, order a copy of your credit report from the three major credit reporting agencies Experian, TransUnion and Equifax. See section "Obtaining a Free Copy of Your Credit Reports" in Chapter 1 for more details.

EXAMPLE: (on next page)

(Month Date, Year)
Annual Credit Report Request Service
P.O. Box 105281
Atlanta, GA 30348-5281

To Whom it May Concern:

Please send me my free annual credit report for all 3 bureaus, Equifax, Experian and TransUnion as I am entitled to receive these once a year.

Thank you,
(Signature)
(Your Name)
(Address)
(City, State, Zip)
(Social Security Number)
(Date of Birth)

After you have received your report(s), it is time to begin the process of clearing up your credit. Remember this process will take time, but it will ultimately benefit you. Stick with it and never give up.

Below is an actual Experian credit report for you to use as an example to follow the steps that I have outlined for you, using the number system and explanation that follows each number. It will guide you on what each account is and how to look at your credit report accurately to determine what is needed to dispute your credit reports accurately. Also, you will know what to look for on your report and determine which legal document you will need to mail.

```
Experian                  Prepared for          Report Date      Page 3 of 8
A world of insight                                                April 23, 2009
                          Report Number         www.experian.com/disputes
                          1434026300
```

Credit Items

---

[1] ZALES/CBSD   Date Opened   Date of Status   Type   **[2]** Status: Account charged off
P.O. BOX 689183   Sep 2004   Jun 2008   R $1,033 written off $733
DES MOINES IA   Reported since Last Reported   Terms past due as of Apr 2009
No phone number available Sep 2004   Apr 2009   1 mo   **Account History**: Charged
Partial account Number   off as of Apr 2009.
60352510866....   **[3]** This account is scheduled
                                                               To continue on record until
                                                               Oct 2014

[4] CIT BANK/DFS   Date Opened   Date of Status   Type   **[5]** Status: Account charged off
12234 N. IH 35 SB   Nov 2004   Apr 2009   R $1,361 written off $527 past
NEWPORT NEWS VA 23606   Reported since Last Reported   Terms Apr 2009
No phone number available May 2007   Apr 2009   NA   **Account History**:
Partial account Number   Charged Off as of Apr
7945012902871.....   2009

---

1. The account holder (Zales/CBSD)

2. The status of this account: notice it is a "charge off" (April 2009)

3. The date the credit bureau will remove this account. (Oct 2014)

4. The account holder (CIT BANK/DFS)

5. The status of this account: notice it is a "charge off" (April 2009)

Experian	Prepared for	Report Date	Page 4 of 8
A world of insight			April 23, 2009
	Report Number	www.experian.com/disputes	
	14340269300		

Credit Items

CIT BANK/DFS (continued)

60 Days past due as of Dec 2008
[6] This account is scheduled to continue on record until Sep 2015

---

[7] **HFC**
P.O. BOX1547
CHESAPEAKE VA
No phone number available
Partial account Number
6804120016....

Date Opened: Jan 2007
Reported since: Aug 2008
Date of Status: Sep 2008
Last Reported: Apr 2009
Type: R
Terms: 1 mo

[8] Status: Account charged off
$11,809 written off $15,730 past due as of Apr 2009
Account History: Charged off as of Aug 2008.
[9] This account is scheduled To continue on record until Oct 2013

---

[10] **CREDIT CONTROL CORP**
11821 ROCK LANDING DR
NEWPORT NEWS VA 23606
No phone number available
Partial account Number
2090201344

Date Opened: Jan 2009
Reported since: Mar 2009
Date of Status: Mar 2009
Last Reported: Apr 2009
Type: C
Terms: 1 mo

[11] Status: Collection
account $87 past due as Apr 2009
[12] This account is scheduled to continue on record Until Sept 2015

Original Creditor: **COX COMMUNICATIONS LAS VEGAS**

---

6. The date the credit bureau will remove this account. (Sept 2015)

7. The account holder: (HFC)

8. The status of this account: Notice it is a "charge off" (April 2009)

9. The date the credit bureau will remove this account. (October 2013)

10. The collection agency: (CREDIT CONTROL CORP)

11. The status of this account: (April 2009 when the collection company received it.)

12. The date the credit bureau will remove this account (April 2009)

13. The original creditor for this collection company # 10

Experian	Prepared for	Report Date	Page 5 of 8
A world of insight		April 23, 2009	
	Report Number	www.experian.com/disputes	
	143026300		

Credit Items   Continued

---

14 CREDIT CONTROL CORP Date opened Date of Status Type   **15 Statue**: Collection account
11821 ROCK LANDING DR   Jan 2009   Mar 2009   C $271 past due as of Apr
NEWPORT NEWS VA 23606   *Reported since Last reported*   Terms   2009.
No phone number available   Mar 2009   Apr 2009   1 mo   **16 Account History:**
Partial account number   Collection as of Apr 2009
2090201345   This account is scheduled
                                                                                                                To continue on record until
                                                                                                                Sept 2015

17 Original creditor: COX COMMUNICATIONS LAS VEGAS

---

18 HSBC BANK   Date opened Date of Status Type   **19 Statute**: Transferred, closed
P.O. BOX 5253   Oct 2006   Jul 2008   R $669 written off
CAROL STREAM IL 60197   *Reported since Last reported* Terms   **Account History:**
No phone number available   Nov 2006   Jul 2008   Charged Off as of Jul 2008
Partial account number   150 days past due as of May
540791502571   2008

20 Sold to: ARROW FINANCIAL   **21 Comment:** "Account information
                                                                                                Disputed by consumer.
                                                                                                This item was verified and
                                                                                                Updated on Apr 2009.

---

14. The collection agency: (CREDIT CONTROL CORP)

15. The status of this collection account: (April 2009 when the collection agency received it)

Disputes with Credit Bureaus | 107

16. The date the credit bureau will remove this account. (Sept 2015)

17. The original creditor: (COX COMMUNICATION) for this collections.

18. The original creditor: (HSBC BANK)

19. The status of this account: (Transferred, closed, written off)

20. Sold to: (ARROW FINANCIAL)

21. Notice there is no date when it will be deleted from the credit bureau.

Now, let's work on this particular report step by step (follow the number sequence.) I chose to dispute every account on this Experian report because this client didn't remember having any of these accounts. This is an ideal report because it has:

- Original creditors
- Collection companies
- A sold account

Experian Dispute Letter

The following Experian dispute letter I am using is to be used as an example for you to follow. It will demonstrate how to accurately dispute a credit report. This will give you a visualization of a credit report as well as how to dispute the accounts, that is listed on this particular credit report. Your own personal credit report will have different accounts listed.

See disputes documents at the end of this chapter for documents that pertain to your credit reports.

(Month, Day, Year)
Experian
P.O. Box 9701
Allen, TX 75013

To Whom It May Concern:

Thank you for my report; however, there are account(s) listed below that are reporting incorrectly. I have no recollection of having these accounts. Please correct these issues and mail a corrected copy of my report to me. The accounts listed below are not mine.

- Zales/Cbsd   # 603525108622   # (1)
- Cit Bank/DFS   # 7945012902871   # (4)
- HFC   # 6804120016   # (7)
- Credit Control Corp # 2090201344   # (10)
- Credit Control Corp # 2090201345   # (14)
- HSBC Bank   # 540791502571   # (18)

Thank you,
(Signature)
(Name)
(Address)
(City, State, & Zip)
(Social Security Number)
(Date of Birth)

Instructions:

Do not place the "# (00)" next to the account number. This is strictly for your reference to follow along to show you where I was getting my information on the report.

Use this form letter, filling in your own information. Don't worry if on your own report you accidentally dispute an account that is yours. Remember, it is up to the credit bureau to verify this account and remove it if it is not verified. Sometimes, even if the account *was* yours, it can be removed earlier than the original date set by the credit bureau.

Print and mail this dispute to Experian, making sure to make a copy for yourself and document your personal file that you have sent a dispute on this particular date to this credit bureau.

After you have completed this step, you are now ready to move forward with the next step.

Collection Agency Accounts

Because you have collection accounts that you have already included in the dispute document to the credit bureaus, you will now need to do the following:

- The Cease and Desist (C&D) document is in Chapter 3. You will need a separate C&D for each collection company.
- If you have multiple accounts for the same collection company that is attempting to collect a debt from you, you can use only one C&D document, making sure to list all the accounts with the collection company.

- Send a C&D document directly to each collection agency, listing one or more accounts.

- Once it receives this demand from you, it will have the option to delete this account from your bureau reports and stop contacting you.

- In most cases, you only will need to send the C&D document once to the collection agency. **Note:** Do this only once for each collection agency, regardless if it's on all three credit bureau reports. Keep your log on all documents sent, so you will not duplicate the letters going out.

- If you have another credit report that has different collection accounts listed, then you will need to send a C&D document to the new collection companies.

Debt Validation and Verification Letter #1

(Month, Date, Year)

Credit Control Corp

11821 Rock Landing Dr

Newport News, VA 23606

RE: Account (# 2090201344)

For: (Cox Communications)

    (# 2090201345 Cox Communications)

To Whom It May Concern:

I have just received a copy of my credit report and noticed an account from your company on it. Please validate this account, according to FCRA §611, part B, subsection (iii) & FDCPA 623 according to Federal standards.

1. Proof that the collection agency was assigned the debt and has the legal authority to collect on behalf of the creditor.
2. Complete payment history.
3. Copy of the original signed agreement or application.

Please validate this information and correct it with any credit bureaus to whom you have reported adverse information about my credit rating. If the information cannot be validated, please delete the account from my credit reports and *cease and desist with all collection efforts.*

Please inform me of the result of your validation within 5 days. Your immediate attention to this matter is appreciated.

Sincerely,

(Signature) (Your name only with no address)

cc: State Attorney General

FDCPA

Instructions:

Fill in only your name. You won't need to put in your address unless you would like to, because this company already has your name and address on file. Sometimes the collection agency does not have your current address if you have moved since you opened the account from the original credit. So make sure not to give it to them.

Do this same process for each separate collection account listed.

Now you need to print and mail this document to your collection company. Also, be sure to document this letter in your log, showing that you have already addressed this particular collection company with the reference account numbers.

It is important to log all documents sent, because accounts will be sold to other collection agencies, making it difficult for you to keep up with which collection agency is trying to collect for which original account holder.

You will sometimes find that two different collection companies are trying to collect for the same original account holder.

By keeping a good log, you will be able to see right away if this is happening. If you do find that a collection agency is collecting for the same debt, go to Chapter 3 and use the Cease and Desist document for "A collection company collecting for the same debt"...

EXAMPLE: (on next page)

Debt Validation Verification Letter #2

(Month, Day, Year)

(Collection Company)

(Address)

(City, State, Zip)

RE: Account (# 0011122)   For: (Original Creditor)

To Whom It May Concern:

I have just received a copy of my credit report and noticed an account

from your company on it. Please validate this account, according to FCRA §611, part B, subsection (iii) & FDCPA 623 according to Federal standards.

4. Proof that the collection agency was assigned the debt and has the legal authority to collect on behalf of the creditor.

5. Complete payment history.

6. Copy of the original, signed agreement or application.

Please validate this information and correct it with any credit bureaus to whom you have reported adverse information about my credit rating. If the information cannot be validated, please delete the account from my credit reports and *cease and desist with all collection efforts.*

This account is also listed with: 2nd collection company. You cannot collect for debt that is being collected by another company.

Please inform me of the result of your validation within 5 days. Your immediate attention to this matter is appreciated.

Cc: State Attorney's General
FDCPA
Sincerely,
(Signature)
(Your Name Only)

Sometimes you will see the end results in both collection companies sending you a letter that they are removing this account from your credit reports.

Keep a copy of this letter for your file, and you also will need to mail a copy of all correspondence such as this to each credit bureau to make certain the collection account does in fact deleted it.

Use the normal dispute document from each of the credit bureaus listed at the end of this chapter. It is the document that lists only the accounts that are not yours—similar to the document you used in the aforementioned example. You will dispute both collection companies from whom you received the notice from that they are each going to deleted their account. Make sure to attach a copy of the letter from each collection company.

Now, the credit bureaus, to whom you send the dispute document and collection letter stating that they are going to remove the account, will send you a new, updated report reflecting that they have, deleted both of these accounts from your credit report within a 45-day period so you can be certain they have been deleted.

Lastly, let's go back to the sample credit report we were working on earlier.

Notice for account #18 HSBC BANK on your sample credit report that this account was transferred, closed and written off. At this time, all you can do is dispute this account because there is no account holder yet. Notice it was sold to Arrow Financial. You will need to wait until you receive a letter from Arrow Financial letting you know that it has purchased your account from the original account holder HSBC BANK. Once you have received this letter, you will mail them a Cease and Desist letter requesting that it stops all collection attempts.

Congratulations! You have just completed the process for your first report.

OTHER NEGATIVE ACCOUNTS ON YOUR CREDIT REPORT

What to do when you have any of the following listed on your credit reports

- Late payments
- Charge off
- Public Records… Bankruptcy, Tax Liens…etc
- Repossession of a vehicle
- Student Loans

1. If you have an account that is yours, and the creditor is reflecting that you have **paid late** (meaning you paid the payment after a 30-day period has passed), the original creditor will put a 30-day late on your credit report, causing your credit score to decrease. Don't panic! There is hope! You will need to dispute this account, using the correct dispute document listed at the end of this chapter. You will dispute this account as "Never paid late." **Remember:** It is up to your original creditor to keep good records to prove this.

    a. Send either **"Forgiveness of Late"** or **"Verification of Late"** document (See Chapter 5: Asking for Forgiveness of Late) to your original creditor at the same time you are disputing the validity of this account with the credit bureaus.

    Note: I had a co-worker who knew the late payment was legitimate but accidentally disputed the account as "Never paid late"—when in fact she had. She was surprised when the original account holder hadn't kept good records and could not prove the account was ever paid late. The result was astounding; it was updated on her credit reports to reflect "paid as agreed, never late." She increased her own credit score.

    b. Do your best to dispute the accounts that you have never paid late. Some accounts on your credit report might be reflecting that you paid a particular account either 30, 60 or even 90 days late, which you do not remember paying late. Most people do not always remember when they paid an account and mistakes do happen. You will be working to get any of your late payments removed from your credit reports.

2. You have an account reflecting on your credit report **"Charge off."** This is common on credit reports, but don't worry. A charge off simply means that the amount of the debt is unlikely to be collected. This occurs when a consumer becomes severely delinquent on a debt. Traditionally, creditors will make this declaration at the point of six months without a payment.

A charge off is one of the most adverse factors that can be listed on a credit report. While a charge off is considered to be "written off as uncollectable" by the original creditor, the debt is still legally valid and remains as such after the fact. Legally, the original creditor has the right to collect the full amount for a certain amount of years, depending on your state for the statute of limitations. (See Chapter 4 for the statute of limitations for your state)

Some creditors that charge off an account will sell the account to an outside collection agency for it to collect the debt. (See Chapter 3 about collection agencies)

Disputing an account that is reflecting a charge off is no different than disputing any other account listed on your reports.

   a. Simply list the account under the accounts that are not yours or that you do not remember ever having. Remember: It is up to the original creditor to prove the account is yours.

   b. By the way, if you do remember that the account is actually yours but you forgot about it, don't worry if you dispute it this way as not your account.

    c. If the account is found by the original creditor, the bureaus will send back an updated report reflecting either the account was "Deleted" or "Verified."

3. **Public Records** are usually listed on a credit report in the following categories: "Tax Lien," "Child Support," "Judgment," "Bankruptcy" and "Foreclosure."

Public records are not normal, everyday accounts such as credit accounts. *Public records are listed on your credit reports but not placed on your reports from any of public agencies.* Yes, you read this correctly.

How do the credit bureaus get this information? It is an open, public record that is filed in a court house. The credit bureaus employ agents who go to the courthouse daily for the filings that appear in the records that day. Because the records publish your name, address, date of birth and social security number, the agent simply gathers this information to take back to the credit bureau he/she works for and then proceeds to place this damaging information on your personal credit report. When a public record is placed on your reports, it is meant by the credit bureaus to remain on your credit reports from 7 to 10 years.

Credit bureaus must verify the information with the courts, as this is the procedure with any dispute sent from a consumer to the credit bureaus. The bureaus will verify the information.

Contact any court house to verify the procedure they use.

To remove these accounts, contact a competent attorney to have these records sealed from public viewing. Also, there is a Sealing of Records document at the end of this chapter if you want to attempt to do it yourself.

After the sealing of the records process has taken place, you will then have the option to dispute these accounts with the credit bureaus. During this process, the credit bureaus will attempt to verify the information from the public record, because they must verify the validity of any disputed debt from a consumer's report. With the records sealed, they will not be able to locate and view the documents. Therefore, the accounts will be removed from your reports.

Note: My friend once accidentally disputed a public record account as, "No knowledge of account," and to her surprise, it was completely deleted.

4. **The repossession of a vehicle** is not what we thought would happen when we made this major purchase, but unexpected events happen in our lives.

   Most companies that lend money on an auto purchase use the vehicle as collateral. This means if you don't make your payments for a period of 90 days, the financial institution has a legal right to take back the vehicle. It can sell it at an action to recover as much money as it can on the money lent to you when you signed your finance contract. But, this can have a serious affect on your credit.

You have an option to work out a payment arrangement with your financial institution to pay off the balance it was unable to collect during the auction. If you choose this method, it will then mark your credit as, "Repossession Paid." This means you will have no collection calls from the financial institution or collection agency (in case the original creditor sold the account to a collection agency).

If your repossession account holder sells your account to a collection agency, then the normal collection procedures for collection agencies apply. (See Chapter 3 Collection Agencies). The normal dispute procedures apply as well.

5. **Student Loans** are given by the U.S. government while someone is attending college to further his/her education with the cost of tuition, books and other financial obligations. This is definitely a loan you do not want to default on as the government will use various means to collect. It will secure the money owed to it, even if it means garnishing your wages or government tax return.

You can dispute the loan as not being yours because the amount is incorrectly reported and the credit bureaus must be reporting this information accurately. Then while your dispute is going through, you should contact your lender, requesting it verify the debt and reflect the accurate amount owed. (See Chapter 6 on Student Loans)

What to do When Your Credit Reports Come Back from the Credit Bureaus

When you receive your "updated" report from the credit bureaus (usually around 45 days from the date the bureau receives your dispute), you will notice on the first page of each report the deleted items. For this example, I will use a TransUnion report so you will understand how to view and work from it correctly.

As you will notice on this particular report, we are going to examine many different accounts such as:

- Bankruptcy Chapter 7
- Bankruptcy Chapter 13
- How accounts in bankruptcy are reporting
- How they should be reporting
- How Released Tax Liens are reporting
- What documents are to be used

See example report on the next page:

TransUnion
Example form
Not an actual report

05/16/2009

Our Investigation of the dispute you recently submitted is now complete. The results are listed below.

If our investigation has not resolved your dispute, you may add a 100-word statement to your report.
If
you provide a consumer statement that contains medical information related to service providers or medical procedures, then you expressly consent to TransUnion including this information in every credit
report we issue about you.

If there has been a change to your credit history resulting from our investigation, or if you add a Consumer statement, you may request that TransUnion send an updated report to those who received Your report within the last two years for employment purposes, or within the last one year for any other
purpose.

If interested, you may also request a description of how the investigation was conducted along with the
Business name, address and telephone number of any company we may have contracted for information.

Thank you for helping ensure the accuracy of your credit information. (copied from an actual report)

Investigation Results

ITEM	DESCRIPTION	RESULTS
ZALE/CBSD	# 6035251086221525	PREVIOUSLY VERIFIED
GMAC PHOENIX ADMIN CTR	# 61908486034	VERIFIED, NO CHANGE
CAPITAL ONE BANK USA	# 4862362374510249	PREVIOUSLY VERIFIED
HOUSEHOLD FINANCE	# 68041200166733	NO LONGER ON FILE
DELL FINANCIAL SERVICES	# 79450129028718172	PREVIOUSLY VERIFIED
ARROW FINANCIAL SERVICES	# 43023322	PREVIOUSLY VERIFIED
LITTON LOAN SERVICING	# 18804963	DELETED
NEW CENTURY SERVICIING	# 1003106249	DELETED
CAPITAL ONE	# 6258899541	VERIFIED, NO CHANGE
EMC MORTGAGE CORP	# 5690003475431	DELETED
ALLSTATE ADJUSTMENT	# 155763622944	DELETED

```
*** 203928143-004 ***
P.O. Box 2000
Chester, PA 19022
                                                    04/12/2009    TransUnion.


P0R78L00201248-i00p069


Ilulululluuluullululluulluulululluululllulu


Our investigation of the dispute you recently submitted is now complete. The results are listed below.

If our investigation has not resolved your dispute, you may add a 100-word statement to your report. If
you provide a consumer statement that contains medical information related to service providers or
medical procedures, then you expressly consent to TransUnion including this information in every credit
report we issue about you.

If there has been a change to your credit history resulting from our investigation, or if you add a
consumer statement, you may request that TransUnion send an updated report to those who received
your report within the last two years for employment purposes, or within the last one year for any other
purpose.

If interested, you may also request a description of how the investigation was conducted along with the
business name, address and telephone number of any company we may have contacted for information.

Thank you for helping ensure the accuracy of your credit information.

                            Investigation Results

ITEM                              DESCRIPTION              RESULTS
CHAPTER 13 BANKRUPTCY DISMISSED   DOCKET #770962           VERIFIED, NO CHANGE
RELEASE OF TAX LIEN               DOCKET #K2008PG3501      VERIFIED, NO CHANGE
STATE TAX LIEN                    DOCKET #K2008P37693      NEW INFORMATION BELOW
RELEASE OF TAX LIEN               DOCKET #2008PG10485      VERIFIED, NO CHANGE
CHAPTER 7 BANKRUPTCY DISCHARGED   DOCKET #874587           VERIFIED, NO CHANGE
WASHMTL/PROV                      # 4479485000100179       NEW INFORMATION BELOW
GEMB/JCP                          # 6008893361909348       VERIFIED, NO CHANGE
HSBC BANK                         # 5407915016555184       NEW INFORMATION BELOW
HSBC BANK                         # 5486975015825582       NEW INFORMATION BELOW
GEMB/JCP                          # 3301509346             NO LONGER ON FILE ──→ *
CAPITAL ONE BANK USA NA           # 529107174996298O       VERIFIED, NO CHANGE
CAPITAL ONE BANK USA NA           # 529107180225961O       VERIFIED, NO CHANGE
FIRST PREMIER BANK                # 5176007736081256       VERIFIED, NO CHANGE
DSNB/MACYS                        # 4800760246790          VERIFIED, NO CHANGE
BANK OF AMERICA                   # 6501000331535O         VERIFIED, NO CHANGE
HOUSEHOLD FINANCE                 # 68648000147202         NEW INFORMATION BELOW
```

The deleted accounts are a permanent, not temporary, fix. These accounts were deleted from the original source; therefore, they will usually never be put back on. Even if you have an account that you cannot send a legal document to, but you believe the account is not yours, you can also dispute the account as "Not mine" or "No knowledge of account." There is a good chance the account will be deleted, because the original creditor did not keep good records of your account to verify that the account does, in fact, belong to you.

How to get More Accounts Deleted the Second Time Around

Now that you have seen results from your first go round with the disputing process, you can re-dispute again to possibly get more accounts deleted. On the new updated report, you again will do the same process you did on the first go round.

You will dispute all the accounts remaining as either "Not mine," "No knowledge of account" or "Never paid late"—whichever the case might be for your credit situation.

1. Send the dispute document that pertains to your situation. You can put as many accounts on one document as you would like. There is no limit to the amount of accounts you can list.
2. If you need to send a second document such as "Cease and Desist" again to all your collection companies listed on your report, do it and remember to document it in your records.
3. Once again, you will have to wait for another 45 days to see the results from re-disputing your credit reports.

Let's begin by using the TransUnion credit report that has now come back after the 45 day period. I will once again explain how the process works and what you can do using your own credit report.

```
                              File Number:    201645366
                              Page:           1 of 3
                              Date Issued:    05/07/2009   TransUnion
```

Public Records
The following items obtained from public records appear on your report. You may be required to explain public record items to potential creditors.

[1] ARKANSAS FED COURT-FAYET Docket #: 874587

FEDERAL BUILDING   **[2] Type**: CHAPTER 7 BANKRUPTCY DISCHARGED   **[3] DateFiled**: 11/2008
35 E. MOUNTAINS   **Court Type**: U.S. BANKRUPTCY COURT   **Responsibility**: Liable
FAYETTEVILLE, AR   **Date Paid**: 02/2009   **Plaintiff Attorney**: Joe
(479) 582-9800   **Assets**: $0

[4] Estimated date that this item will be removed: 10/2018

[5] ARKANSAS FED COURT-FAYET Docket #: 770962

FEDERAL BUILDING   **[6] Type**: CHAPTER 13 BANKRUPTCY DISMISSED   **[7] Date Filed**: 04/2007
35 E MOUNTAINS   **Court Type**: U.S BANKRUPTCY COURT   **Responsibility**: Liable
FAYETTEVILLE, AR   **Date Paid**: 04/2007   **Plaintiff Attorney**: Pro
(479) 582-9800   **Assets**: $0   **Liabilities**: $0

[8] Estimated date that this item will be removed: 03/2014

[9] BENTON COUNTY CIRCUIT CO Docket #: 2008PG104785

100-102 NE A STREET   **[10] Type**: RELEASE OF TAX LIEN   **[11] Date Filed**: 07/2008
BENTONVILLE, AR 72712 **Court Type**: CIRCUIT COURT   **Responsibility**: Individual
(479) 271-1015   **Date Paid**: 08/2008   **Plaintiff**: State of Arkansas

[12] Estimated date that this item will be removed: 07/2015

1. Arkansas Fed Court-Fayet is the name of the original creditor.

2. This reflects that this particular account is listed as a Chapter 7 *discharged* bankruptcy.

3. The date of this bankruptcy filing

4. The estimated date that this item will be removed, which is 10 years from the date of the filing in the courthouse.

5. Arkansas Fed Court-Fayet is the name of the original creditor

6. This reflects that this particular account is listed as a Chapter 13 *dismissed* bankruptcy.

7. The date of this bankruptcy filing
8. The estimated date that this item will be removed, which is seven years from the date of the filing in the courthouse.
9. Benton County Circuit Court is the name of the original creditor.
10. Type of account is a "Released" Tax Lien
11. The date of this filing.
12. The estimated date that this item will be removed, which is seven years.

Listed for #1 is Arkansas Federal Court, which is reflecting a Chapter 7 discharged bankruptcy. A discharged bankruptcy means it was in fact filed and followed through until completion and discharged by the bankruptcy judge. All debts have been forgiven and no longer due as they have been brought to a zero balance. Usually a Chapter 7 bankruptcy will remain on your credit reports for a period of no more than 10 years.

Listed for #5 is Arkansas Federal Court, which is reflecting a Chapter 13 dismissed bankruptcy. A dismissed bankruptcy means this bankruptcy was not completed until finalized by the judge. It is as though this bankruptcy was never filed. Notice the credit bureau still placed this bankruptcy on the credit report where it can remain for only seven years.

Listed for #9 is Benton County Circuit Court, which is reflecting a released tax lien. A released tax lien means this debt, owed to the IRS, has been paid in full. Notice it can remain on a credit report for a period of seven years from the date it was paid in full, not from the date it was filed.

Now lets move on to the next part of this updated TransUnion credit report:

File Number: 201645366
Page: 3 of 3
Date Issued: 05/07/2009   **TransUnion**

Consumer Credit Report continued:

13 FIRST PREMIER BANK # 5178007736081258

3820 N. Louise Ave
Sioux Falls, SD 57107
Phone number not available

Balance:
Date Verified: 03/2009
High Balance: $690

15 Pay Status: Unrated
Account type: Revolving
Responsibility: **Individual**
Date Opened: 07/2007
Date Closed: 08/2007
Date Paid: 08/2007

Loan Type: Credit Card
14 Remarks: CHAPTER 7 BANKRUPTCY
Estimated date that this Item will be removed: 07/2014

16 GEMB/JCP # 6008893361509346

P.O. Box 981402
El Paso, TX 79998
(800) 541-0800

Balance:
Date Verified: 05/2009
High Balance: $0
Credit Limit: $0

18 Pay Status: Payment after
Charge off/ collection
Account Type: Revolving
Date Opened: 10/2005

17 Loan Type: CHARGE ACCOUNT
Remarks: CHAPTER 7 BANKRUPTCY
Estimated date that this Item will be removed: 03/2015

19 HSBC BANK # 5407915016555184

P.O. Box 5253
Carol Stream, IL 60197
(800) 477-6000

Balance:
Date Verified: 10/2008
High Balance: $934
Credit Limit: $0

21 Pay Status: Payment after
Charge off, Collection
Account Type: Revolving
Responsibility: Joint

20 Loan Type: Credit Card
Remarks: Acct Info Disputed By Consumer
Estimated date that this Item will be removed: 03/2014

22 HSBC BANK # 5488975015825592

P.O. Box 5253
Carol Stream, IL 60197

Balance:
Date Verified: 04/2008
High Balance: $ 1,585

24 Pay Status: Payment after
Charge off/ Collection
Account Type: Revolving

23 Loan Type: Credit Card

---

128 | *"The Legal Method" To Clearing Your Own Credit*

13. Original creditor First Premier Bank

14. Reflects it was filed in a Chapter 7 bankruptcy

15. The status of this account is showing that it is "unrated"

16. Original creditor Gemb/JCP

17. Reflects it was filed in a Chapter 7 bankruptcy

18. The status of this account is showing that it is in a charge off/collection account.

19. Original creditor HSBC Bank

20. Shows the account is disputed by consumer (meaning you)

21. The status of this account is showing that it is in a charge off/collection account.

22. Original creditor HSBC Bank

23. Shows the account is disputed by consumer (meaning you)

24. The status of this account is showing that it is in a charge off/collection account.

The credit bureau has just mailed its updated credit report to you with their findings of each account. You may be very confused and wondering what to do with, but there are still documents you can use to continue to work on your credit file to get more accounts deleted.

Let's take a look at numbers #1, Arkansas Federal Court, #5 Arkansas Federal Court and #9 Benton County Circuit Court.

Send a "Seal of Records" document to each courthouse with the hopes the courthouse will seal the public records of each account. Once the records are sealed, when the credit bureaus try to locate these records, they will no longer be available to verify as they will no longer be public records for viewing.

Notice on this example document that I have accounts #1 and #5 on the same document. Because it is going to the same courthouse address, I have placed both docket numbers for each case. I did not need to send a separate document for each account.

For #9 I used a separate document because it was going to a different address.

REQUEST TO SEAL RECORDS

(Month, Day, Year)
Arkansas Federal Court
Federal Building
35 E. Mountains
Fayetteville, AR 72701
Re: Case # 874587   (#1)
          770962   (#5)

To Whom It May Concern:

I have been informed that a record in my name is held by your office are open for public viewing, as well as being displayed over the internet. I have no record of this account. Please verify that this in fact my account.

Identity theft is a problem in our country; I believe it starts with issues such as this.

I am requesting in writing to have this record sealed from public viewing if it is in fact proved to be mine. This record would then hold my personal information, which I choose not to have released to the public.

If I need to complete a legal package to have this record sealed, I will be happy to do this. Please let me know what package and forms I will need to do this. Is this a "motion to vacate" form?

Please send me in writing your decision in this matter and proof these are my accounts.

Thank you,
(Signature)
(   )
(   )
(   )

Request to Seal Records

(Month, Day, Year)
Benton County Circuit Co   (# 9)
100-102 NE A Street
Bentonville, AR 72712
Re Case # 2008PG10485

To Whom It May Concern:

I have been informed that a record in my name is held by your office is open for public viewing, as well as being displayed over the Internet. I have no record of this account. Please verify that this in fact my account.

Identity theft is a problem in our country; I believe it starts with issues such as this.

I am requesting in writing to have this record sealed from public viewing if it is in fact proved to be mine. This record would then hold my personal information, which I choose not to have released to the public.

If I need to complete a legal package to have this record sealed I will be happy to do this. Please let me know what package and forms I will need to do this. Is this a "motion to vacate" form?

Please send me in writing your decision in this matter and proof these are my accounts.

Thank you,
(Signature)
(   )
(   )
(   )

For #13 for First Premier Bank, you will notice this account was filed in a Chapter 7 bankruptcy, and it is being rated as "unrated" (see #15). This means this account is not hurting your credit score as it was included in the bankruptcy. You will want to get this account completely removed from your credit report as a bankruptcy is already listed on your report in the public records section (see #1). It is reflecting your bankruptcy.

For #16 GEMB/JCP, this account also was filed in the Chapter 7 bankruptcy only. According to #18, the status is reflecting that it has not been filed in the bankruptcy and is an active collection account. This generally means it is hurting your credit score and has been placed with a collection company that soon will be sending you a notice that your account was received from GEMB/JCP for collections. You will need to send GEMB/JCP a document telling them this account has been filed in your bankruptcy. Below is an example document to use. You also will need to dispute this account with the credit bureau as it is reporting the status as "incorrect." Later in this chapter, I will give you an example of how this is accomplished.

For #19 HSBC Bank, this account was in fact filed in the Chapter 7 bankruptcy, but is not reflecting as such according to #20. Notice also with #21, the pay status is reflecting it as a charge off/collection account. With this on your report, it will definitely hurt your credit score and possibly cause this account to be sold to a collection company that will then be contacting you often because it will want a payment on this account (see Chapter 3 about the practices of a collection company). You will need to dispute this account with the credit bureau because it is reporting incorrect. You also will need to contact HSBC Bank, to remind them that this account was in fact filed in the Chapter 7 bankruptcy and to update this account with all credit bureaus to whom they are reporting this account.

This is the same method applies for #22 the other account listed for HSBC Bank

See example document below regarding this account.

If you did not know what to look for on a report, you would not know that all this could actually be reporting incorrectly and would need your expertise to correct it.

Now let's begin with using the correct document to send to HSBC Bank to have this error corrected immediately.

Listed below is the correct document you will need to use and mail to them.

This document is used for # 16

Month, Day, Year
Gemb/ JCP
P.O. Box 981402
El Paso, TX 79998
RE: (Account 6008893361509346)

Dear Manager:

I had an account with your company that unfortunately, due to a situation beyond my control, I was unable to meet my debt obligations. This left me no choice but to file bankruptcy.

This account is now filed in my Chapter 7 bankruptcy, which was dismissed on (Date); therefore, you are reporting this account in error as it is not a collection account.

Please remove this account from any and all bureaus you report to as it is reporting in error.
Thank you,
(Signature)
Your Name
Address
City, State, Zip

This document is used for # 19

Month, Day, Year
HSBC Bank
P.O. Box 5253
Carol Stream, IL 60197
RE: Accounts (#5407915016555184....
   54889750158/25592)

Dear Manager:

I had an account with your company that, unfortunately due to a situation beyond my control, I was unable to meet my debt obligations. This left me no choice but to file bankruptcy.

This account is now filed in my Chapter 7 bankruptcy, which was dismissed on (Date); therefore, you are reporting these accounts in error as they are not collection accounts.

Please remove these accounts from any and all bureaus you report to as it is reporting in error.

Thank you,

(Signature)
(Your Name)
(Address)
(City, State and Zip

With having your documents completed, You can now document in your journal the accounts that you are sending so you will have them for future reference.

Now it is time to address the credit bureau with the issues of accounts that are not reporting correctly. Below is an example of a credit dispute form you would use for these particular accounts listed on the sample TransUnion report. Your own personal accounts will vary on which document you will use.

(Month, Day, Year)

TransUnion

1561 E. Orangethorpe Ave

Fullerton, CA 92831

To Whom It May Concern:

After having my credit run, it has come to my attention that accounts that are not mine are reporting on my report. Please remove the accounts listed below:

- Arkansas Fed Court   # 770962   (#5)
- Benton County Ciruit Co   # 2008PG10485   (#9)
- First Premier Bank   # 5178007736081258   (#13)

The accounts listed below were included in my Chapter 7 bankruptcy that was dismissed on (Date: See #3 for date of discharge). Please update these account to reflect as such. These accounts listed below were included in a bankruptcy and therefore, should not be reflecting on the credit report, because they are included in the "Public Record" section on the credit report. I am requesting these accounts be deleted.

- GEMB/JCP   # 6008893361509346   (# 16)
- HSBC Bank   # 5407915016555184   (# 19)
- HSBC Bank   # 5488975015825592   (# 22)

Sincerely,

(Signature)

(Your Name)

(Address)

(City, State, Zip)

Now that you have worked on Experian and TransUnion reports, let's look at the last report, Equifax. By showing you examples and how to work on different credit reports, you should not have a problem reading and working on your own credit reports. The most common issue with credit is that many Americans are not able to read and understand their own credit reports—let alone work on them correctly.

Let's take this Equifax and work from it. You will notice it has a completely different format to read and understand.

> **EQUIFAX**
> **CREDIT FILE: JULY 9, 2009**
> **Confirmation # 91610472365**
>
> Dear Someone:
>
> Below are the results of your request for Equifax to reinvestigate certain elements of your Equifax credit file. Equifax contacted each source directly and our investigation is now completed. If you have any additional questions or concerns, please contact the source of that information directly.
>
> You may contact Equifax regarding the specific information contain in this letter within the next 60 days by visiting us at www.investigate.equifax.com or by calling a Customer Representative as (888) 800-7426 from 9:00 am to 5:00 pm Monday-Friday in your time zone. If you want to request a free copy of the Equifax credit file you can call our toll free number at (877) 576-5766.
>
> **The Results Of Our Reinvestigation**
>
> **1.** >>> We have reviewed your concerns and our conclusions are: **DELETED ACCTS**
> The following disputed accounts are currently **not reporting on your credit file**: chase/418586690259, Citibank/dfs/7945012908871, feb/frys/504926649002 and gemb/jcp/336136. The additional disputed accounts are not currently reporting on the Equifax credit file.
>
> **Collection Agency Information (This section includes accounts that have been placed for collection with a collection agency...**
>
> **2.** >>> We have researched the collection account. Account # - 2090201345 The results are: Equifax **verified** that this item belongs to you. (Shows it was Verified)
> Credit Control Corp: = **COLLECTION COMPANY** Collection Reported 07/2009 Assigned 01/2009: Creditor Class – Cable/ Cellular: Client: Cox Communications = **ORIGINAL CREDITOR**.
>
> **3.** >>>We have researched the **collection account**. Account # 2090201344. Equifax **verified** that this item belongs to you.
> Credit Control Corp is the collection company(**Original Creditor**) COX COMMUNICATIONS

#1 is the area that states which accounts have been deleted. Notice on this particular report there are four deleted accounts.

- Chase   #418586690259
- Citi Bank   #7945012908871

- Feb/Frys   #504926649002
- Gemb/Jcp   #336136

#2 is a collection account that has been verified

- Credit control #2090201345 with the original creditor: Cox Communications

3 is a collection account that has been verified

- Credit Control #2090201344 with the original creditor: Cox Communications

Let me remind you that this report had already been disputed 45 days earlier. So keep in mind, as you are reading and learning about what to do with a report, that it has just come back to you from the credit bureau.

In the first part of this report, notice in Section #1 that this is the area that will let you know what accounts have been updated or deleted. Notice that there are, in fact, deleted account. Did you think that when you disputed 45 days earlier, these four accounts would actually be deleted? This is why it is so important to be able to work on your own reports. You don't always need someone to do it for you or leave the accounts to just come off sometime in the future by themselves.

An updated report from the credit bureau will automatically be sent to you after a dispute. You do not have to worry about re-ordering it to see if any accounts have been deleted.

#2. This is a collection account from Credit Control Corporation, a debt collector company that has bought the account from Cox Communication. Cox Communication was the original creditor who was unable to collect the fee's owed to them. Notice how the credit bureau informs you that the account has been researched and is verified in the first line under, "We have researched the collection account and it is in fact your account."

3 This is a collection account from Credit Control Corporation, a debt collector company that has bought the account from Cox Communication. Cox Communication was the original creditor who was unable to collect the fee's owed to them. Notice how the credit bureau informs you that the account has been researched and is verified in the first line under, "We have researched the collection account and it is in fact your account."

You don't remember having an account with Credit Control Corp because you have not signed a contract ordering service from it. Don't worry, you can do something about both #2 and #3.

> Send this account a Cease and Desist document. You can use one document, placing both accounts and account numbers on it (see Chapter 3 for this document).

CEASE AND DESIST

(Month, Day, Year)
Credit Control Corp   (#2) & (#3)
11821 Rock Landing Dr
Newport News, VA 23606-4207
Re: Account # (2090201345)   Company: (Cox Communications)
           # (2090201344)   Company: (Cox Communications)

To Whom It May Concern:

In accordance with the Fair Debt Collection Act §1692g, I hereby request that you validate these debts. The act provides that you shall cease collection of the debt, or any disputed portion thereof, until you obtain verification in accordance with the law, that verification must be in writing and contain a copy of a judgment (if applicable), and the name and address of the original creditor and supporting evidence of the alleged debt.

If you are collecting on any debt, I am requesting that you send me a copy of my original application or sales agreement, so that I can identify my signature.

I am also requesting you cease communication with me for all purposes and remove any derogatory reporting to whom all credit bureaus you report to.

According to the Fair Debt Collection Practices Act, Section 805 law.

Sincerely,

(Signature)

(Your Name Only)

Now that you have filled out and sent your document, it would be a good idea to also send a dispute to Equifax, letting them know these accounts are not yours. With sending the Cease and Desist, the collection company generally should not verify this account, causing it to be deleted from Equifax. Equifax will send you a new, updated report reflecting any changes from this dispute within 45 days from them receiving it.

Next is an example dispute form to use:

(Month, Day, Year)
Equifax
P.O. Box 105314
Atlanta, GA 30348

To Whom It May Concern:

After receiving my credit report it has come to my attention that accounts that are not mine are reporting on my credit file. These accounts are listed below:

Please remove these accounts and send me an updated report.

- Credit Control Corp   # 2090201345
- Credit Control Corp   # 2090201344

Thank you,
(Signature)
(Your Name)
(Address)
(City, State, Zip)

By now, you should have an understanding of the process and be able to read your reports and know what situations to look for. If there are small mistakes listed on your reports, it is your responsibility to look for them and correct. If you are not going to take care of this, no one else will.

When you're your credit report is run while trying to make a credit purchase and your application is turned down, you will have a clear understanding what to look for.

ONCE A CREDIT REPORT COMES BACK REFLECTING THAT ALL ACCOUNTS HAVE BEEN VERIFIED.

Next is an example of a TransUnion report that has been disputed twice and accounts are still reflecting as "verified," meaning the credit bureau has already received your disputes and contacted each creditor listed on your dispute letter.

Take a moment to look at this report because it is different than the normal credit report. TransUnion is letting you know that the accounts have been verified and there is nothing more you can do except add a consumer statement of 100 words or less to your credit report. Notice this statement is in the following letter. The letter also lists the accounts it is referring to for your viewing. Don't lose hope. You still have one last chance to clear up more accounts using another type of validation document instead of a dispute document.

> **TransUnion**
> Example form   05/16/2009
> Not an actual report
>
> Thank you for contacting TransUnion. Our goal is to maintain complete and accurate information on consumer credit reports. We have provided the information below in response to your request.
>
> Re: Dispute Status
>
> Our records show that your creditor(s) previously verified as accurate the ttems that are listed below. Therefore, under the Fair Credit Reporting Act, we consider this dispute frivolous and we will not reinvestigate the item(s) unless you can provide court papers or a recent, authentic letter from the creditor(s) that explains what information should be updated.
>
> If you disagree with the results of your dispute, you may add a consumer statement of 100 words or less to your credit report or you may contract the creditor directly. If you provide a consumer statement that contain medical information, then you expressly consent to TransUnion including this information in every credit report we issue about you.
>
> The names and addresses are listed below:
>
> ARKANSAS FED COURT-FAYET
> DOCKET # 770962
> FEDERAL BUILDING
> 35 E. MOUNTAINS
> FAYETTEVILLE, AR 72701
> (479) 582-9800
>
> BENTON COUNTY CIRCUIT CO
> DOCKET # 2008PG3501
> 100-102 NE A STREET
> BENTONVILLE, AR 72712
> (479) 271-1015
>
> BENTON COUNTY CIRCUIT CO
> DOCKET # K2008PG7693
> 100-102 NE A STREET
> BENTONVILLE, AR 72712
> (479) 271-1015

You will now be challenging the credit bureaus directly. They will have to absolutely prove it is your account or delete it.

1. You will dispute once again, only this time you will be using a different document specifically for the credit bureaus. The use

of this document is only after you have already disputed each credit bureau twice.

2. The credit bureaus will now be responsible to prove the account is actually your account by sending you proof of your documents with each of your creditors.

3. Most original account holders either still have the account in their computer or they have sent it to an outside source, such as a collection agency. n most cases, the records are lost in all the transfer, so there are times that the credit bureaus are unable to secure a copy of the documents you are requesting.

You will find an example of this document on the next page. This is a dynamite document for you to enforce your legal rights with the credit bureaus for accurate reporting.

(Month, Day, Year)

TransUnion

P.O. Box 2000

Chester, PA 19022-2000

To Whom It May Concern:

This letter is a formal request for the description of the procedures used to determine the accuracy and completeness of the disputed information, including the business name, address, and telephone number of any furnisher of information contacted in connection to this reinvestigation, in compliance with the Fair Credit Reporting Act, section 611, part B, subsection (iii)

§611. Procedure in case of disputed accuracy 15 U.S.C. §1681 (i) (6) (B) Contents. As part of, or in addition to, the notice under subparagraph (A) a consumer reporting agency shall provide to a consumer, in writing before the expiration of the 5 day period referred to in subparagraph (A)

- iv. a statement that the reinvestigation is completed;
- v. a consumer report that is based on consumer's file as that file is revised as a result of the reinvestigation;
- vi. a notice that, if requested by the consumer, a description of the procedures used to determine the accuracy and completeness of the information shall be provided to the consumer by the agency, including the business name and address of any furnisher of information contacted in connection with such information and the telephone number of such furnisher, if reasonable available;

I am disappointed that you have failed to maintain reasonable procedures to assure complete accuracy in the information you publish, and insist you comply with the law by providing the requested information within the 15 days allowed.

As a matter of convenience to you and to expedite my request, I am re-submitting my request to correct my credit report.

The account(s) listed below are not my accounts:

- Arkansas Fed Court   # 770962
- Benton County Circuit # K2008PG3501
- Benton County Circuit # K2008PG7693

Please give this letter the attention it deserves.

(Signature)
(Your Name)
(Address)
(City, State, Zip)
(Social Security Number)   -   -
(Date of Birth)   -   -

Congratulations! You have completed the entire dispute process of all credit bureaus regarding accounts listed on your reports.

CHAPTER 10

Inquiry Removal

INQUIRY REMOVAL

Most bureaus will report inquiries on your credit report for a period of two years. If you have inquiries listed on your credit report that you don't recall ever applying for, you are entitled to dispute these inquiries. If they are deleted from your report, this will increase your score. Most people can't remember every creditor to whom they had applied; therefore, do your best, even if you put down a company you might have applied with.

1. It is the responsibility of the credit bureaus to keep accurate records. If they feel this is a valuable and correct inquiry, they will keep it on your report.

2. If you know you did not apply to a particular company, you are entitled to write to the company directly for it to prove your inquiry did it fact happen by your request.

3. Once you have requested proof from the creditor and it has mailed you a confirmation or denial letter, send a copy of the confirmation to the credit bureaus to get this inquiry deleted from your credit report.

4. When a company runs a credit inquiry on you, it will notice how many other inquiries have been run on you. If there are more than a certain amount per month, and no new accounts have been opened, they will assume you are a high credit risk as you have too many inquiries. This is why you will want to make sure your credit inquiries are completely accurate.

Earlier I used example reports for you to see how disputing reports was done. Now, I will show you example reports so you are able to see how to dispute inquiries on each credit bureau.

```
Experian              Prepared for        Report Date    Page 16 of 22
A world of insight                        April 23, 2009
                      Report Number       www.experian.com/disputes
                      211488662
```

Record of requests for your credit history
We made your credit history available to your current and prospective creditors and employers as showed by law. Experian may list these inquiries for up to two years so that you will have a record of the companies that accessed your credit information.

Inquiries shared with others
[1.] The section below lists all of the companies that have reviewed your credit report as a result of an action you took such in applying for credit or financing or as a result of a collection. The inquiries in this section are shared with companies that view your credit history.

	Date:	Reason:
[2.] **CAPITAL ONE AUTO FIN** P.O. BOX 30281 SALT LAKE CITY, UT 84130	May 30, 2009	[3.] Permissible purpose. This inquiry is scheduled to continue on record until Jun 2011.

	Date:	Reason:
[4.] **CHASE** P.O. BOX 30144 ALBUQUERQUE, NM 87190	May 30, 2009	[5.] Permissible purpose. This inquiry is scheduled to continue on continue on record until June 2011.

1. Notice in this section it details inquiries and how they can remain on your credit and are viewed by other companies who run a credit report on you.

2. Capital One Auto Fin is the company that ran this report to see if it was able to open an account for you.

3. It is reflecting that this inquiry was run for permissible purposes and it is scheduled to continue being placed on your credit record for two years. You will see by the date, it was run on May 30, 2009, and it will continue on record until June 2011.

4. Chase is the company that has placed an inquiry on your report.

5. It is reflecting the same for # 3.

This is how you will read the section of inquiries for your Experian report.

Now lets look at the Experian in the section that does not hurt your credit score.

```
Experian                    Prepared for        Report Date      Page 17 of 22
A world of insight                              April 23, 2009
                            Report Number       www.experian.com/disputes
                            211488662

                                                Inquiries shared only with you.
Garcia Honda              Reason:               You may not have initiated the following
8301 LOMAS BLVD NE        Auto Loan             inquiries, so you may not recognize each
ALBUQUERQUE, NM           This inquiry is       source.
                          Scheduled to
                          Continue on
                          Record until
                          Feb 2011      6. These Inquiries do not effect your credit score
                                        CARMEL FINANCIAL CORP      Aug 22, 2009
                                        101 E CARMEL DR STE 200
                                        CARMEL IN 46032


                                        CAP ONE                    Apr 14, 2009
                                        P.O. BOX 30281
                                        SALT LAKE CITY, UT


                                        WACHOVIA DEALER SVCS       May 30, 2009
                                        23 PASTEUR
                                        IRVINE, CA  92618
```

These inquiries do not affect you credit score.

> 6. Notice Carmel Financial Corporation only has a date of when the inquiry was run on April 22, 2009.

These inquiries do not have to be disputed because they are not impacting your credit report at all. They will generally fall off your report in time.

TRANSUNION REPORT

```
                         File Number:    208542085
                         Page:           9 of 10
                         Date Issued:    07/04/2009   TransUnion
```

Consumer Credit Report continued:

[1] Regular Inquiries
The following companies have received your credit report. The inquiries remain on your credit report for two years.

[2] ARVEST BANK
913 W. MONROE
P.O. BOX 799
LOWELL, AR 72745
(501) 750-6919

[3]. Requested On: 06/01/2009   Inquiry Type: PARTICIPANT

[4] ARVEST MORTGAGE
8250 MACON RD
CORDOVA, TN 38018
(901) 685-7599

[5] Requested on: 07/13/2007   Inquiry Type: PARTICIPANT

6. Promotional Inquiries:
The companies listed below received your name, address and other limited information about you so they could make a firm offer of credit of insurance.

BARCLAYS BANK DELAWARE   Requested On: 11/2008
125 SOUTH WEST STREET
WILMINGTON, DE 19801

BARCLAYS BANK DELAWARE   Requested On: 08/2008
125 SOUTH WEST STREET
WILMINGTON, DE 19801

JPMORGAN CHASE BANK   Requested On: 09/2008
800 BROOKSEDGE BLVD
WESTERVILLE, OH 43081

#1 In this section the report clearly states Regular Inquiries. This will let you know this is the section you will be working on because these inquiries are impacting your credit score in a negative way.

#2 Arvest Bank is the company that requested a credit file on you.

#3 shows the date this request was ran on it also shows you the Inquiry Type: participant

#4 Arvest Mortgage is the next company that requested a credit file on you.

#5 shows the date this request was run. It also show you that it was, in facts a credit transaction.

#6 Notice these inquires are only Promotional Inquiries that do not impact your credit score.

When you are disputing a TransUnion report for the inquiries, make sure you are only working on the inquiries that are impacting your credit score.

EQUIFAX REPORT

```
EQUIFAX                                EXAMPLE CREDIT REPORT
CREDIT FILE: # July 8, 2009            NOT AN ACTUAL REPORT
CONFIRMATION # 9161047265

Credit Report Continued:
```

[1.]

Inquiries that display to companies (may impact your credit score)
This section lists companies that requested your credit file. Credit grantor may view these requests when evaluating your credit worthiness. Employment Inquiries do not impact your credit score.

Company Information	/ Inquiry Date(s)
[2.] The Hertz corporation City, OK 73134-2606	**[3.]** 07/11/2009
[4.] ARVEST MORTGAGE COMP 5520 Macon Rd Ste 2 Cordova, TN	**[5.]** 12/08/2008
Avis Budget Car Rental 300 Centre Pointe Dr Virginia Beach, VA	09/30/2008

You have seen that all credit bureau reports are not the same but you will now have an idea of what to look for and what to do.

#1 is the inquiry display box letting you know these inquiries may impact your credit score. When you see this box, you will know that the accounts listed below this box are the inquiry accounts you will need to work on to have removed.

#2 The Hertz Corporation is the company that has run this inquiry

#3 Notice this inquiry was run on 07/11/2009 and 03/26/2008. Therefore it is effecting your credit two times.

#4 This is another company Data Facts Inc: Arvest Mortgage Company

#5 It was run on 12/08/2008

Simply follow the guidelines, read all reports effectively and fill in the correct dispute form for each credit bureau to get your inquiries deleted from your report permanently.

Next we will look at the example inquiry removal you can use to get most inquiries deleted from your reports before the two-year period is completed.

(Month, Day, Year)
Experian
P.O. Box 9701
Allen, TX 75013

To Whom It May Concern:

Thank you for sending my credit report; however, after reviewing it, I noticed inquiries listed that I did not authorize. Please remove these inquiries:

- (Now list each inquiry with bullets like you see me writing in this area.
- List each account by name, notice there is no account number
- Also notice you can keep adding as many inquiries as you like.)

Thank you,
(Signature)
(Your Name)
(Address)
(City, State, Zip)
(Social Security Number)
(Date of Birth)

Now you are finished with the completed process of working on credit reports as well as inquiries.

You are on your way to a brighter credit future with the knowledge you now possess—you will even able to help others.

Congratulations!

Forms

Use this form to Order you credit reports:

Annual Credit Report Request Service
P.O. Box 105281
Atlanta, GA 30348-5281
Month, Date, 200

To Whom It May Concern:

Please send me my free annual credit report for all 3 bureaus, Equifax, Trans Union and Experian as I am entitled to receive these once a year.

Thank you,
Name:
Address
City, State, Zip
Phone (   )   -
Social Security Number: -   -
Date of Birth: -   -

> *Use this document to dispute the IRS account.*

Credit Bureau
Address
City, State, Zip

, 200

To Whom It May Concern:

After having my credit ran while attempting to purchase a home it has come to my attention that accounts that are not mine are reporting on my report. Please remove these accounts listed below:

- List your accounts with the I.R.S. along with the account number.

Thank You,
You're Name
Address
City, State, Zip
Social Security Number: -   -
Date of Birth: -   -

Use this document to dispute accounts that are not yours or you have no recollection of the account along with accounts that have never been paid late. Always dispute accounts to the best of your knowledge as mistakes sometimes happen. Sometimes you will dispute an account as not yours even though it is; you made a mistake because you just didn't remember the account, and don't worry the credit bureau will verify the account and correct your report. You might even notice that even though it is your account the credit bureau might even delete the account from your credit report. Remember human errors do happen. It is up to the credit bureaus to prove the account and report accurately.

Credit Bureau
Address
City, State, Zip
Month, Date, Year

To Whom It May Concern:

Thank you for my report however there are account(s) listed below that are reporting incorrectly. Please correct these issues and mail me a corrected copy of my report. The accounts listed below are NOT mine.

- List the account   # 123654   putting in the account number

The account(s) listed below have never been paid late.

- List the account   # 123655

Thank you,
You're Name
Address
City, State, Zip
Social Security Number: -   -
Date of Birth: -   -

Use this document to dispute accounts that have never been paid late. The credit bureaus will check with the account holder to make sure this account is being reported accurately. The account holder will have to prove you paid the account late. If they don't keep accurate records and you dispute the account as never being paid late, you will see your credit report updated to reflect paid on time. The late payments will be updated to reflect paid/never late. Remember it is up to the original account holder to prove you paid the account late if it is going to remain on your report.

Credit Bureau
Address
City, State, Zip
Month, Date, Year
RE: Report #

To Whom It May Concern:

After having my credit ran while attempting to purchase a home it has come to my attention that accounts that are not late and have never been late are reporting on my report. Please update these accounts listed below:

- List the account   # Put in the account number

Thank You,
You're Name
Address
City, State, Zip
Social Security Number: -   -
Date of Birth: -   -

Use this document when disputed account was previously deleted and came back on, It sometimes will happen.

Credit Bureau
Address
City, State, Zip

, 200

To Whom It May Concern:

After having my credit ran while attempting to purchase a home it has come to my attention that an account that is not mine and was once removed from my credit report, is now appearing on my report.

Please remove this account listed below:

-

Enclosed is my previous report showing the deleted account: which needs to be deleted immediately.

Thank You,
Social Security Number: -   -
Date of Birth: -   -

Use this document to update the credit bureaus the account in paid in full and being reported in error.

Credit Bureau
Address
City, State, Zip

▓▓▓▓▓ ▓▓▓▓▓ , 200▓

Dear Credit Bureau,

Enclosed is a receipt proving this account is paid in full.

This is a list for your records of which account(s) I am referring to:

- ▓▓▓▓▓

Now that this account has been paid in full please remove any derogatory information regarding this account since this account has been paid in full.

Please send me my current credit report so I can see the change on my report. Also

I have been denied credit after having my credit report ran through factual data.

Thank you for your cooperation,
Social Security Number: ▓▓▓ - ▓▓ - ▓▓▓▓
Date of Birth: ▓▓ - ▓▓ - ▓▓▓▓

> *Use this document to dispute your accounts as not yours as your social security number was used illegally.*

EQUIFAX
P.O. BOX 105314
ATLANTA, GA 30348

_____, 200___

Report Number:

To Whom It May Concern:

After having my credit ran while attempting to purchase a home it has come to my attention that accounts that are not mine are reporting on my report. Please remove these accounts listed below:

- List you account   # List the account number
- List your next account   # List the account number

The accounts listed below are not from a creditor I never signed a contract with. I have no knowledge of these accounts. Please remove these accounts listed or prove with a copy of a signed contract that I owe this company.

My social security number should not be held with these companies according to the: social security privacy act (S-324), (the privacy act of 2001) and (Section 502 of the Gramm-Leach-Bliley Act 15 U.S.C. 6802) along with the Financial Services Modernization Act. ("facilitates criminal activity and can result in a significant invasion of individual privacy.")

- List your account   # List the account number

Thank You,

Name

Address

City, State, Zip

Social Security Number: ███ - ██ - ████

Date of Birth: ██ - ██ - ████

> Use this document to list accounts that are not your, never been paid late, and inquiries, You can list as many accounts that you need to on one sheet so you only have to mail 1 document to each credit bureau.

Credit Bureau Name
Address
City, State, Zip
Month Date , 200

To Whom It May Concern:

After having my credit ran while attempting to purchase a home it has come to my attention that accounts that are not mine are reporting on my report. Please remove these accounts listed below:

- List the account   # 1111222
- Another account   # 1125522

The account(s) listed below have never been paid late:

- List the account   # 1236547
- List another is you have one # 112255

The Inquiries listed below I did not authorize, please remove:

- List the inquiries

Thank You,
Your name
Address
City, State & Zip
Social Security Number: -   -
Date of Birth: -   -

> *Use this document to dispute all inquires that you don't remember applying for credit with.*

Credit Bureau
Address
City, State, Zip
Month, Date, Year
Report Number:

To Whom It May Concern:

Thank you for sending my credit report, however after reviewing it I noticed inquires listed that I never gave authorization for, Please remove these inquiries:

-

Thank You,
You're Name
Address
City, State, Zip
SS#   -   -
D.O.B   -   -

> Use this document to send directly to each creditor who has placed an inquiry on your credit report.

Company who made the inquiry
Address
City, State, Zip
RE: Account: Inquiries

To Whom It May Concern:

After having my credit report ran an inquiry from your company was listed. I don't recall ever giving my permission for this inquiry.

I believe this inquiry from your company was put on my credit report by mistake. This inquiry is hurting my credit score, **would you please remove this inquiry from my credit report**. I do understand that under normal conditions inquiries usually remain on a credit report for up to two-years.

I do understand you can make the decision to remove it earlier than normal. There is no legal document stating exactly how long this will remain on my credit report. I am asking you to forgive this inquiry as this was not intentional as I don't remember giving permission for it.

Thank you,
You're Name
Address
City, State, Zip

> *Use this document to dispute all inquires that you don't remember applying for credit with.*

Credit Bureau
Address
City, State, Zip
Month, Date, Year
Report Number:

To Whom It May Concern:

Thank you for sending my credit report, however after reviewing it I noticed inquires listed that I never gave authorization for, Please remove these inquiries:

-

Thank You,
You're Name
Address
City, State, Zip
SS#   -   -
D.O.B   -   -

> *Use this next validation document if you have already disputed the accounts with the credit bureaus and you know for sure the accounts are not yours or you believe they are not yours.*

Credit Bureau
Address
City, State, Zip
Month, Date, Year

To Whom It May Concern:

This letter is a formal request for the description of the procedures used to determine the accuracy and completeness of the disputed information, including the business name, address, and telephone number of any furnisher of information contacted in connection to this reinvestigation, in compliance with the Fair Credit Reporting Act, section 611, part B, subsection (iii)

§611. Procedure in case of disputed accuracy 15 U.S.C. §1681 (I) (6) (B) Contents. As part of, or in addition to, the notice under subparagraph (A) a consumer reporting agency shall provide to a consumer, in writing before the expiration of the 5 day period referred to in subparagraph (A)

i. a statement that the reinvestigation is completed;
ii. a consumer report that is based on consumer's file as that file is revised as a result of the reinvestigation;
iii. a notice that, if requested by the consumer, a description of the procedures used to determine the

> accuracy and completeness of the information shall be provided to the consumer by the agency, including the business name and address of any furnisher of information contacted in connection with such information and the telephone number of such furnisher, if reasonable available;

I am disappointed that you have failed to maintain reasonable procedures to assure complete accuracy in the information you publish, and insist you comply with the law by providing the requested information within the 15 days allowed.

As a matter of convenience to you and to expedite my request, I am re-submitting my request to correct my credit report.

The account(s) listed below are not my accounts.

- [redacted]

Please give this letter the attention it deserves.

You're Name
Address
City, State, Zip
Social Security Number: [redacted] - [redacted] - [redacted]
Date of Birth: [redacted] - [redacted] - [redacted]

> *Use this document if someone you know has passed away. This will prevent others from using their social security number. This is always a good idea to send.*

Credit Bureau

Address

City, State, Zip

Month, Date, Year

To Whom It May Concern:

I just wanted to let you know that my wife/husband _____ has passed away on _____ _____, 2006.

Name

Address

City, State, Zip

Social Security Number: _____ - _____ - _____

Date of Birth: _____ - _____ - _____

If someone was to run credit or a credit inquiry on her that her credit file will reflect "deceased."

Enclosed is a copy of his/her death certificate.

If you should need anything further from me please feel free to contact me at the address below. Please send me confirmation of your receipt of this issue.

Thank you,

Name of family member sending in this document

Address

City, State, Zip

www.ingramcontent.com/pod-product-compliance
Lightning Source LLC
Chambersburg PA
CBHW020949230426
43666CB00005B/238